fragile ecologies

fragile ecologies

Contemporary

Artists'

Interpretations

and

Solutions

Barbara C. Matilsky

RIZZOLI
NEW YORK

in association with
The Queens Museum of Art,
New York

This publication was prepared in conjunction with the exhibition *Fragile Ecologies: Artists' Interpretations and Solutions* by Dr. Barbara C. Matilsky for The Queens Museum of Art. The exhibition was developed for circulation by the Smithsonian Institution Traveling Exhibition Service (SITES).

Exhibition Tour
September 15–November 29, 1992: The Queens Museum of Art, Queens, New York
February 6–May 2, 1993: Whatcom Museum of History and Art, Bellingham, Washington
May 16–August 29, 1993: San Jose Museum of Art, San Jose, California
December 4, 1993–January 30, 1994: Madison Art Center, Madison, Wisconsin
February 18–April 10, 1994: De Cordova Museum and Sculpture Park, Lincoln, Massachusetts
April 30–July 3, 1994: Center for the Fine Arts, Miami, Florida

Major funding for the exhibition has been provided by The Rockefeller Foundation and The Nathan Cummings Foundation, with additional public support from the New York State Council on the Arts.

The Queens Museum of Art is housed in the New York City Building, which is owned by the City of New York, and its operation is supported in part with public funds provided by the New York City Department of Cultural Affairs and the office of the Queens Borough President Claire Shulman. Additional support is provided by corporate and foundation donors, individual members, the New York State Legislature, and the New York State Council on the Arts.

Published by
Rizzoli International Publications, Inc.
300 Park Avenue South
New York, New York 10010

92 93 94 95 96 / 10 9 8 7 6 5 4 3 2 1

Printed in Hong Kong

Library of Congress Cataloging-in-Publication Data
Matilsky, Barbara C.
     Fragile ecologies: contemporary artists' interpretations and solutions / Barbara C. Matilsky
          p. cm.
     "Prepared in conjunction with the exhibition . . . for the Queens Museum of Art"—T.p. verso.
     Includes bibliographical references and index.
     ISBN 0-8478-1592-7
     1. Art, American—Exhibitions. 2. Environment (Aesthetics)—Exhibitions. 3. Nature (Aesthetics)—Exhibitions. 4. Art, Modern—20th century—United States—Exhibitions. I. Queens Museum of Art. II. Title.
N6512.M35 1992   92-15771
704.9'43—dc20   CIP

Peace in Place reprinted by permission of Sterling Lord Literistic, Inc.
© 1979 by Amiri Baraka

Excerpt from poem "Green-Backed Firecrown" from *Art of Birds* by Pablo Neruda, translated by Jack Schmidt.
© 1985 University of Texas Press

Photo, title page and page 59, courtesy JPL/NASA

On the cover: Agnes Denes, *Wheatfield, Battery Park City — A Confrontation*, 1982.
1.8 acres of wheat planted and harvested, New York City

Design by Douglas & Voss Group, New York

Contents

I WOULD LIKE TO THANK all of the artists featured here, many of whom have worked with me since 1988, when the idea for the book and exhibition was conceived. Just as their work is based on collaboration so, too, does *Fragile Ecologies* represent a collaborative effort with the artists who answered my questions and provided me with documentation. I am especially grateful to Helen Mayer Harrison and Newton Harrison, who advised me during this project.

Fragile Ecologies would not have become a reality were it not for the generous support of the following people who believed in its concept and philosophy: Tomas Ybarra-Frausto, Associate Director of the Arts and Humanities, the Rockefeller Foundation; Joan Shigekawa, Program Director for the Arts, and Charles R. Halpern, President, the Nathan Cummings Foundation.

I am also grateful to the staff at the Queens Museum of Art for its consideration and support, which enabled me to work uninterrupted on this manuscript. Steven Klindt, Director, granted me the rare freedom to work exclusively on this project; and Phyllis Bilick, Assistant Curator, temporarily assumed many additional curatorial responsibilities, made photographs, and provided encouragement and good cheer each morning. Dawn Giegerich, Registrar, enthusiastically advised on illustrations; and Joana Vicioso, Curatorial Secretary, helped with many details in assembling the manuscript. David Freilach, Development Officer, and Danielle Amato Milligan, Director of Development, helped secure funding. Sharon Vatsky, Curator of Education, and Lorraine Klagsbrun, Assistant Curator of Education, developed the education component of the exhibition. Marc H. Miller discussed many ideas with me during the early stages of the project, and the enthusiasm of Louis Grachos and Connie Cullen were important sources of support.

My thanks go as well to Crisley McCarson, Project Director at the Smithsonian Institution Traveling Exhibition Service (SITES), who was a wonderful partner while coordinating the exhibition for production and touring; and Roderick Frazier Nash, Professor of Environmental History at the University of California at Santa Barbara, who first introduced me to the notion of environmental ethics in his book *The Rights of Nature: A History of Environmental Ethics*.

I appreciate the cooperation of the private collectors, museums, and galleries who agreed to lend art to the exhibition and to provide photographs for the book. Special thanks go to Marc Nochella, Susan Young, and Ronald Feldman at Ronald Feldman Fine Arts, who were always encouraging and gave me access to their photo archives, answered questions, and helped me with research. The following people also provided me with valuable information: George Adams of Frumkin/Adams Gallery; Jay Belloli; Peter Boswell, Associate Curator at the Walker Art Center, Minneapolis; Agnes Denes; Nina Felshin; Hans Haacke; Peggy Holmes, Visual Arts Coordinator, King County Arts Commission, Washington; Jeff Levine at the John Weber Gallery; Jill Manton, Director, Public Art Program of the Arts Commission of San Francisco; John Hallmark Neff; Amanda Schaeffer of Stephen Wirtz Gallery; and Bonnie Sherk.

Adele J. Ursone, Editorial Director at Universe Publishing/Rizzoli International, made the publishing process a pleasure because of her enthusiasm for the project and her knowledge of art. She sensitively selected Kay Douglas and Tom Voss, who interpreted the spirit of the book in a thoughtful and innovative design. James Stave, Editor, graciously coordinated the editorial production of this book.

Acknowledgments

I thank Anna Noll, who made the time to read the first draft of the manuscript in the middle of her own deadlines.

During the long hours of formulating ideas and writing, I looked to Michelle Rutman and Jyoti Duwadi for guidance, support, and creative inspiration. By sharing the philosophy that pervades this book, they helped keep me balanced. They read the manuscript and made significant contributions. Mr. Duwadi also advised me during all phases of the exhibition's organization. I dedicate this book to them, to the artists in the exhibition, and to all who share the belief that the last vestiges of unspoiled nature need protection as our quintessential artistic masterpiece.

Barbara C. Matilsky
New York City, 1992

I OFTEN DAYDREAMED about writing this book in a tiny cottage by the sea or in a cabin surrounded by forested peaks. Instead, I had to be content with an office at the Queens Museum of Art in Flushing Meadows Park, New York City, squeezed in between the Grand Central Parkway and Van Wyck Expressway. It turned out to be a most fitting place. Like many of the sites for artwork discussed in this book, it has been transformed by man. Once a thriving wetland, sheltering a myriad of marsh birds and plants, the site became a landfill where trash was dumped. Later, the land was reclaimed for the Worlds' Fairs of 1939 and 1964. Planted with locust trees, oaks, and pines, it is now the second largest park in New York City. Ironically, the two fairs celebrated the theme of progress, based on total faith in a technology that few suspected would leave massive environmental damage in its wake. Flushing Meadows Park is a perfect example of a fragile ecology. It is a place where nature's balance has been breached and one that depends upon our constant vigilance to ensure its future as an urban oasis. Many of the artists discussed in *Fragile Ecologies* and featured in the exhibition by the same name are attempting to revitalize similar urban waste sites for people and for other forms of life.

Artists are in a unique position to effect such environmental changes because they can synthesize new ideas and communicate connections between many disciplines. They are pioneering a holistic approach to problem solving that transcends the narrow limits of specialization. Since art embodies freedom of thought, spirit, and expression, its creative potential is limitless. Art changes the way people look at reality. In its most positive mode, art can offer alternative visions.

While studying nineteenth-century landscape painting and its relationship to natural history, I first became aware of the artist's ability to translate ideas into images that profoundly influence public perceptions of nature. Paintings by Joseph Mallord William Turner (1775–1851), François-Auguste Biard (1799–1882), and Frederic Edwin Church (1826–1900) enabled students of science to visualize concepts of erosion, glaciation, and other natural forces that contributed to the formation of the planet. Their works also stimulated a heightened appreciation for the earth and its indigenous populations, fostering a cult of travel to remote and remarkable places. European civilization's traditional fear of mountains and other awesome aspects of nature gave way to wonder and experiences of spiritual transcendence. This change in attitude was also sparked by writers and poets such as Johann Wolfgang van Goethe (1749–1832), William Wordsworth (1770–1850), and Walt Whitman (1819–1892), all of whom contributed to a merging of culture and nature during a period of intensifying industrialization.

Recognizing the impact of art on ideas and feelings about nature and alarmed by the deteriorating condition of the planet, I became interested in how contemporary artists were responding to environmental issues. I found many parallels between the landscape painters of the nineteenth century and artists today: both integrate social and natural history, they collaborate with or are influenced by specialists in other fields, and they communicate the wonder of nature to the public. By expanding the tradition of the artist as naturalist, an increasing number of artists are providing solutions to environmental problems.

An understanding of ecology — the interrelationship of all forms of life in their diverse environments — is essential for the survival of the planet. The word derives from the Greek words *oikos*, which means "house" or "habitat," and *logos*, which translates as "doctrine." Although the term originated in 1866, it was not

Introduction

Why is it that all of Gaia dances in

harmony while we humans are the

only ones out of step?

—*Rachel Rosenthal*

(*performing* Pangaean Dreams,

New York City, 1991)

I • Tony Da, *Symbols of the Southwest*, 1970

In *Symbols of the Southwest*, Tony Da, a member of the San Ildefonso Pueblo tribe, interprets this theme of interconnected harmonies. Here, man and woman, bird and animal are abstractly defined and unified within one space. Inspired by ancient Navajo sand paintings, and prehistoric pottery and fabric designs, the artist fuses past and present styles of art and beliefs to celebrate the regenerative forces of nature or, as the wiseman Black Elk described, the community of all living things.

until the 1890s that the first important books on the subject were published. Many contemporaries describe the science simply as "planetary housekeeping." The earth houses a wide range of ecosystems — communities of plants and animals that depend on a particular environment or habitat for life. An ecosystem can be as small as a decaying redwood tree or as large as the Pacific Ocean, and it includes the dense populations of cities. Ecological art attempts to ameliorate one of the critical problems facing the planet: the widening gulf between natural and urban ecosystems.

This study begins with prehistoric art and surveys critical interludes in history — hunting-and-gathering, the emergence of agriculture, the Industrial Revolution — in order to place into perspective art since the 1960s, which forms the book's core. The emergence of ecological art may be understood as part of a long tradition of artists responding to the environment. Keen observers of the natural world, artists throughout history have sought metaphors in nature to help define human existence. During periods characterized by environmental change, artists responded by inventing new genres and imagery to cope with the problems of human survival. Although the forces of "progress" were often against them, they eased the psychological tensions that arose as a schism developed between a reverence for nature and its exploitation.

The first works of art ever created — the cave paintings of western Europe — established harmony between people and animals. Preserving nature's balance has since motivated artists throughout the millennia. Art, ritual, and myth, intricately intertwined until relatively recently, developed in response to this paramount need to secure a sacred connection to the earth. Over the centuries, the relationships between people and nature grew more distant. Since the advent of the Industrial Revolution, this gap has widened. However, many artists, especially landscape painters, continued to maintain the primacy of nature through their art.

Since the late 1960s, an important new art movement has emerged to reestablish a vital link to nature by communicating an experience of its life-generating powers. Artists interpret specific environmental problems, as well as the forces and phenomena of nature. In contrast to earlier artists who mediated a balance between people and nature through painting and sculpture, contemporary artists actually restore or re-create natural ecosystems. Their artworks are located in or near major cities. Landfills, vacant urban lots, rivers, wetlands, the continental shelf — these are all creatively undergoing remediation and reclamation by artists. Not only are many of these sites made inviting for native species of plants and animals, they are conceived as public spaces where people can develop a closer relationship with nature.

Ecological art is rooted not only in nature and the natural sciences but also in the cultural history of a site. Many artists are inspired by Native American cultures, which have long practiced environmental ethics. Tribal beliefs and customs, although differing from group to group, were all based on a harmonious and economically sustainable stewardship of the land. Their ceremonies and myths are spiritual celebrations of nature that connect people to the earth. This type of bonding is essential for establishing respect for the entire community of life (FIG. 1). Native American art, mythology, and beliefs have influenced the theme, content, and imagery of many ecological artworks.

In indigenous cultures, nature centers the members of a group by providing necessary boundaries of behavior, as well as access to the realms of metaphysical enlightenment. The relationship of first peoples to their environment offers industrialized cultures important lessons in communication and psychological and social integration with nature. Paradoxically, the systematic destruction of forests, prairie, tundra, and other habitats also threatens the human inhabitants from whom we have so much to learn.

Although this study focuses on art of the United States, international connections are noted. Despite an emphasis on Western culture, other traditions are acknowledged as enduring models for elevating environmental consciousness. The arts and philosophy inspired by Hinduism, Taoism, Buddhism, and the many forms of animism embrace a unity among all living things. These ideas permeate the work of many contemporary artists, who transcend the expression of individual ego and seek to express a more encompassing and more harmonious ecological order.

In this quest for balance, we must stand rooted like a tree and yet be fluid like the waters. Nature provides us with the essential metaphors for life and an understanding of our existence. The culture we have developed is essentially the sum product of humanity's search for meaning and identity. Ultimately, nature is essential for both cultural blossoming and human survival.

It is the story of all life that is holy

and good to tell, and of us two-leggeds

sharing in it with the four-leggeds

and the wings of the air and all green

things; for these are children of one

mother and their father is one Spirit.

—*Black Elk*

(Holy Man of the Oglala Sioux,

born nineteenth century,

from Black Elk Speaks*)*

Art and the Balance of Nature:

An Historical Overview

What a world

where lotus flowers

are ploughed into a field

—*Issa (Japanese poet, 1763–1827)*

THE PHYSICAL GRANDEUR AND FORCES OF NATURE have always inspired both awe and fear in people. All through the ages, attempts were made to understand and harness its powers for human advantage. From the first prehistoric tools shaped over two million years ago to the current experiments in genetic engineering, humans have modified nature.

As early peoples transformed the environment, they developed spiritual beliefs that mediated a balanced relationship with the earth. A supernatural unity with the world of animals was experienced by hunters-and-gatherers. Agricultural communities venerated the sacred tree and the Great Goddess to ensure continuity of the seasons and fertility of the land. In these preindustrial societies, objects of art dramatized myths and rituals that revolved around the life-generating powers of nature — growth, death, and renewal. To convey the mysterious and sacred essence of the terrestrial and celestial realms, art, as well as dance and music, evolved as an integral part of life. Over the centuries, the intimate relationship previously established between people, animals, and the earth eroded. This estrangement accelerated during the Industrial Revolution. Many artists, however, continued to maintain and communicate the essential bond with nature.

When overlaying environmental history with the history of art, there often exists a striking correlation between changes in the physical environment and the emergence of new art forms and images. Several significant developments in art appear to coincide with periods characterized by environmental stress. Some of the topics examined in this chapter include: the depiction of animals in hunting-and-gathering societies; the image of the sacred tree, sculptures of the Great Goddess, and the introduction of landscape painting during the evolution of agriculture; and the efflorescence of landscape painting and the emergence of photojournalism in the industrialized world.

In the beginning, changes to the landscape were limited in scope and initiated relatively slowly by people living in small populations. By contrast, the rapid pace and global scale of the current destruction of nature is without precedent. Artists, society's most sensitive observers of internal and external realities, can help us to understand and renew our vital connection to the earth.

HUNTING AND GATHERING SOCIETIES: THE SACRED ANIMALS

Fire was prehistoric people's most effective tool in altering the environment and establishing social life. Harnessing the powers of fire for warmth, cooking, and protection cast the hearth as the center of communal living. Used to make tools and to clear forests to increase the visibility of prey, fire expanded man's hunting abilities.[1] It helped relieve early hunters-and-gatherers from the incessant pressures of survival. People could now direct more of their energies inward, and a spiritual awareness of themselves in relationship to nature and their environment emerged.

The individual responsible for the physical, emotional, and spiritual well-being of the group was the shaman, who is still a powerful figure among contemporary hunters-and-gatherers. Shamans are visionaries whose prophetic dreams and powerful sense of intuition, identified at a young age, distinguish and separate them from other members of society. They are responsible for healing, as well as for maintaining the rituals that foster a group's cohesion. Most often, the shaman is also the artist, using objects of art to illuminate the meaning and to heighten the drama of ceremonies (FIG. 2).

The first works of art, painted in manganese and iron-oxide pigments on the walls of caves in western Europe, were created by shamans who sought to perpetuate the spiritual and physical bond between humans and nature (FIG. 3).[2] Dating from almost 25,000 years ago, cave paintings of animals symbolize the sublime forces of nature. The animals — horses, bison, aurochs, mammoths, ibex, red deer — were perceived to possess supernatural properties.

Early peoples, in constant and intimate interaction with nature, recognized the extraordinary powers that set animals apart from them. The strength of the bison, mammoth, and bear; the speed of the red deer and lion; the ability of birds to fly and fish to swim must have inspired a sense of awe and admiration for the very attributes that humans were denied. In the cave paintings, the shaman-artists have captured the essence of these animals, depicting their powerful physiques swelling with vitality. The poses and compositions vary; they are heroically grounded to the earth or endowed with the freedom of agile movement. Through an intense identification with these animals, which embodied the divine forces of nature, it is likely that early man and woman entered into a sacred union with animals and the cosmos.[3]

The caves may have functioned as religious sanctuaries where spiritual beliefs, centered on establishing harmony with nature, especially the animal kingdom, were assimilated by younger members of the group through rites of initiation. The animal images appear to correspond to concepts of balance, fertility, and regeneration. By pairing particular animals, often accompanied by abstract sexual symbols, artists suggested a complimentary division of the world into male and female counterparts similar to the yin/yang philosophy of Taoism.[4] The lessons learned from the cave art and rituals may have guided the group's behavior and inspired a hunting ethic based on preserving the female of the species in order to maintain the stability of the herd.

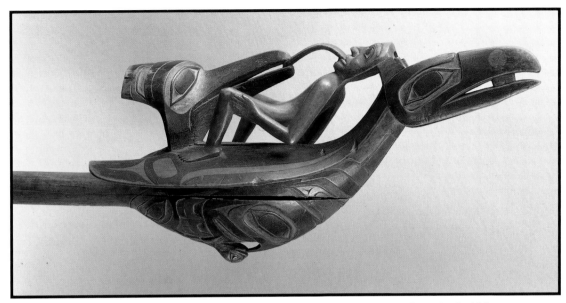

2 • Tlinget, *Raven Rattle*, 19th century

3 • Bison from the Cave of Altamira, Spain, ca. 15,000–10,000 B.C.

Whether through man-made pressures or changes of climate and habitat, some species of large mammals, like the bison, became endangered.[5] Extinctions may have occurred in Europe and northern Asia about 20,000 to 10,000 years ago, coinciding with the great age of cave art.[6] Could these images be a response, along with rituals, to their diminishing numbers? By regarding these animals as sacred, early peoples may have refrained from killing too many of them. The fact that the majority of animals portrayed in caves were only occasionally eaten is perhaps evidence of the respect they were accorded as well as their scarcity.[7] They might have been consumed on the occasion of a sacramental feast at which the animal and human identities merged. Such ceremonies would have further distinguished these animals from ordinary prey.

The reverence for animals in prehistoric times can also be understood by studying the customs and myths of later hunters-and-and-gatherers, whose identification with animals has always been intense (FIGS. 2, 4). The Senufo of Africa and the Tlingets of North America, for example, bonded with particular animals, which anthropologists call "totems." Totemic animals were considered brothers or sisters, and clan members referred to themselves by the animal's name. The spirit or soul of a person was believed to reside in the totemic animal for safekeeping. Death to the animal was believed to result in death to a family member, and thus these animals were rarely eaten. As a system of beliefs, totemism may have helped to balance the ecosystem by maintaining the supply of particular animals.[8]

The ritual veneration of a particular animal or plant also served as a means of fostering identity and communal bonding among members of a clan. Totemism stimulated a wealth of cosmological legends, as the founding ancestor was usually an incarnation of the totemic animal. The worship of animals and the development of totemism thus served spiritual, social, and ecological functions.

On the coast of the American Pacific Northwest, shaman-artists created impressive ceremonial objects that are based almost exclusively on animals (FIG. 2). On raven rattles created by the Tlingets, the intimate connection between people and the animal world is literally depicted, as the shaman lies on the raven's back and puts his tongue into the bird's beak.[9] The infusion of the animal spirit into that of the human would then be transferred to other tribal members during the ceremony where this rattle was used. The raven — a bird believed to have created the sun and the heavens — is abstractly portrayed to convey its spiritual essence. Expressively patterned in bold colors, its body is streamlined to suggest the power of flight. The artist imbues the raven with a fearsome and magnificently commanding presence by emphasizing the eyes and open beak.

The Senufo, living on the Ivory Coast of Africa, identify with the hornbill, emblematic of power and intelligence (FIG. 4). The bird is often depicted pregnant, symbolizing the fertility and continuity of the tribe and the natural world. In this image, the artist synthesizes male and female forms; the elegantly elongated beak, referring to the phallus, dips into a swelling body, which is painted with triangulated waves to suggest feathers and movement. As in the image of the raven, the hornbill is abstractly defined. This merging of abstraction and naturalism is a means by which the artist could capture the spirit of the animal. Stylistically removing the animal from the realities of natural appearance, the artist was able to suggest its sacred aspect.

4 • Senufo, Ivory Coast, Africa, *Bird,*
19–20th century

The Development of Agriculture: The Sacred Tree and the Great Goddess

The environmental changes induced by hunters-and-gatherers were small in comparison to those introduced by agriculture, the next stage of human development. The domestication of plants and animals first originated in southwest Asia 9,000 years ago; it emerged in southeast Asia 8,000 years ago and independently in Meso-America 7,000 years ago. With the advent of agriculture, nature was radically transformed. Society's life-style, religious ideas, and art forms reflected a newly defined relationship between the earth and its human inhabitants.

As agriculture developed, animals such as sheep, goats, oxen, and cows were tamed by people who then became their caretakers (FIG. 5). Herds became the property of particular families or communities, thus establishing the concept of ownership and a more servile relationship of animals to human beings. The animal provided food and clothing, fertilizer for the crops, transportation, power to pull the plow, and a means of trade or barter. As beasts of burden, they were given proper care and attention.

5 • *Sennedjen and his wife plowing and sowing in the field*, Tomb of Sennedjen (detail from East Wall), 19th Dynasty

In some agricultural societies, the animal is still considered sacred. The cow is revered in India where the Hindu religion prohibits its killing. This status evolved from society's need for plow animals and dung for fuel.[10] In southeast Asia, the elephant is also revered and plays an important role in legend and myth. Animals were not killed or used indiscriminately. Even today, in many societies, when animals are killed, a prayer or ceremony of thanksgiving is enacted, intended to appease nature for this trespass of its domain.

Although nature was still worshiped, planting required dramatic alterations to the landscape. Intensive agriculture usually results in soil depletion, and this may have contributed to the collapse of the agricultural civilizations of Mesopotamia and of the Maya in Mexico.[11] During this period of environmental stress in many parts of the world, artists introduced the image of the tree, which reflected creation myths and symbolized the rejuvenation of nature. Art and ritual no doubt served to provide assurances of stability and guidance in these times of hardship.

Agriculture involved clearing forests, leaving behind clusters of trees that probably assumed the status of sacred groves (FIG. 5). In the Egyptian tomb of Sennedjen (Nineteenth dynasty), a painting portrays a husband and wife plowing

6 • *Hathor as tree goddess giving birth to the sun,* ca. 600 B.C.

7 • *Winged beings worshiping the sacred tree, and eagle-headed, winged beings pollinating the sacred tree,* 885–860 B.C.

the earth and sowing seeds. Below this image is a row of date palms, revered by the Egyptians. In such groves, shrines were often erected so that people could communicate directly with the gods and goddesses of nature. (FIG. 12). These groves also functioned as protective habitats for wildlife, since extinction could result from land clearance. During the reign of King As'oka of India almost 2,300 years ago, forests were set aside as preserves for elephants.[12]

The image of the sacred tree in art emerged in Mesopotamia during the fourth millennium, when the introduction of the plow permitted the cultivation of large tracts of land.[13] In the history of art, the sacred tree later appears in Egypt, India, and Meso-America, three other areas in the world where deforestation was rampant.

Depictions of the sacred tree provided a crucial connecting link with origin myths, which celebrated the tree as a source of all life. Worship of the tree is prevalent worldwide — among Native North Americans, ancient Babylonians, Mayans, Aztecs, and early Scandinavians, Indians, and Egyptians.[14] In ancient myths, the tree holds the many layers of the universe together by emerging from deep within the earth and reaching skyward toward the heavens. Firmly rooted in the ground and shedding and growing new leaves each year, the tree symbolizes stability, continuity, and rebirth.

The image of the sacred tree grounded people to the past and fostered a sense of emotional and physical well-being in the present. In many works of art, people receive power and strength from the tree as they reverently acknowledge its force in guiding their destinies (FIG. 6). On a bronze vessel from ancient Egypt, the sun is born from the head of the tree goddess, Hathor, whose physical identity merges with that of the tree. Her body becomes the trunk and her arms one of its many radiating branches. She is the life-force from which the cosmos emerges. The artist

18 • *Offering to a tree*, from Mexican codex, 16th century

portrays two worshipers on either side who hold out their hands to receive her energy and power.[15]

Well aware of its power as symbol, the kings of Assyria may have later appropriated the image of the sacred tree to legitimize their political rule (FIG. 7). In reliefs from the Northwest Palace of Ashurnasirpal II, the king is portrayed in several relief panels along with winged divinities who perform a ritual invoking the sacred tree. The eagle-headed genii pollinate the tree to ensure the survival of both tree and ruler. These images suggest the king's responsibility for administrating the daily rituals required to perpetuate the fecundity of nature, from which came the wealth of his domain.

In Meso-America, rituals associated with the sacred tree were similarly intended to ensure the fertility of plants and trees. A drawing from a Mexican codex, created immediately after contact with Europeans, illustrates a traditional ceremony that survived through the sixteenth century (FIG. 8). Here, the artist exaggerates the fruit of the tree, especially its reproductive parts. The two people who sit beside its flowering branches imbibe and eat in an act of thanksgiving for the bountiful harvest. This image may also relate to the Aztec and Mayan origin myth that describes a flat and multilayered earth resting on five sacred trees — one at the center and four corresponding to the corners or directional loci.[16]

The identification of the sacred tree with the Great Goddess appears in many cultures. On the Vedika Pillar from Bharut in Madhya Pradesh, an Indian goddess symbolizes the life-generating energy of the tree (FIG. 9). As in Egyptian art, the goddess and tree are physically entwined. Her breasts swell like the lush fruit on the branch that she grasps above her head. They form a unified entity whose vitality is communicated by an elegant and sinuous composition.

Rituals and art celebrating the sacred tree represent only one aspect of nature worship that sustained agricultural societies. Art and religion also reflect an inti-

9 • *Vedika pillar with tree goddess*, 100–80 B.C.

10 • *Serpent Goddess* (Priestess?) from Knossos, ca. 1600 B.C.

mate and mystical union between people and the Great Goddess, who embodied the natural cycles of birth and death. Ceremonies in her honor were designed to perpetuate this steady rhythm so necessary for the propagation of crops. Artists created sculptural figurines of the goddess to help communicate with the forces of nature (FIG. 10). Artworks like the Minoan *Serpent Goddess* (ca. 1600 B.C.) from Crete accompanied seasonal rituals invoking abundance and renewal. This sculpture may portray either a goddess or a priestess engaged in a rite in her honor. The wide, staring eyes indicate a trancelike state, an entry into the spirit world. Bare breasted and assuming a commanding posture, she holds snakes in both hands. The serpents may have been part of the ceremony or may symbolize regeneration, since they periodically shed and acquire new skin. Indicating the presence of water, the snake also can be understood as a life-generating force.[17]

The worship of the Great Goddess reflected women's power to perpetuate the species. The earth subsequently became synonymous with and symbolic of the womb. To penetrate, violate, or gouge the earth was blatantly sacrilegious. In recognition of the land's revered status, early miners offered sacrifices, abstained from sexual relations, and fasted before digging into the ground.[18]

The development of agriculture thus bequeathed an organic, nurturing conception of nature; it also sowed the seeds from which blossomed the first cities and civilizations. When wild grains were domesticated and planted in prepared fields, people were able to settle permanently in villages. Surplus harvests, along with milk from domesticated cows, caused increases in population, and this in turn required more land for cultivation, setting off a spiraling cycle that continues to this day.

URBANISM AND THE EMERGENCE OF LANDSCAPE PAINTING

In both China and Europe, the art of landscape painting evolved in conjunction with the growth of cities and expendable wealth. Landscape paintings were as intrinsic to the perpetuation of society's beliefs and values as were the artworks created by hunters-and-gatherers and early agriculturalists. Although divorced from ritual and ceremony, landscape painting reinforced the spirituality of urban dwellers, who were farther removed than their fellow countrymen from the sacred forces of nature. These paintings inspired respect for and an appreciation of nature's vitality. Symbolically, they reconnected people to the land as cities expanded and deforestation accelerated.

By communicating the beauty and revitalizing essence of nature, artists reminded urban patrons of its power, and permitted them to experience it vicariously. The images in landscape paintings represented and symbolized freedom, which contrasted to the confining spaces and daily routine of city life. In Pompeiian villas, artists created magnificent illusions of nature by painting landscapes on walls to simulate natural vistas (FIG. 11). In the *Casa del Bracciale d'Oro*, lush vegetation, wildflowers, and fruit-bearing trees that attract a myriad of birds are composed beneath portraits of the residents. Through careful observation and naturalistic detailing, the artist communicates the density of growth and an atmospheric breadth of space.

The first landscape paintings appeared in Rome during the first century B.C. Their introduction coincides with environmental stress — the overcultivation of land and deforestation, which may have contributed to the decline of both Greece

11 • *Garden with plants and birds, Casa del Bracciale d'Oro*, Pompeii

and Rome.[19] George Perkins Marsh, considered the father of American environmentalism, describes in his seminal book *Man and Nature* (1864) how the cities of Greece and the Roman Empire decimated their forests for shipbuilding, fuel, and agriculture.

The paintings from Pompeii reflect this environmental condition (FIG. 12). Artists often depict a denuded landscape with a religious shrine located in a small forest grove or near a sacred tree. In many works, a figure, accompanied by a goat, approaches the altar in a posture of sacrificial offering. These paintings illustrate the ritual communion with nature that continued to exist in a highly advanced civilization.

Landscape painting also fulfilled the spiritual yearnings of urban patrons in China, where it emerged and evolved as a genre during the eighth through tenth

12 • *Sacro-idyllic landscape with shepherd and goats* (detail), from Pompeii

centuries (FIG. 13). In contrast to the public display of Pompeiian landscapes on building walls, Chinese landscapes were painted on silk scrolls and were designed to be read by unfolding each scene sequentially. This format encouraged an atmosphere of intimacy and private communion with the landscape image. Creating and viewing such works required a state of meditation in which artist and patron were able to perceive the balance and mysteries of nature.[20]

Chinese (and later Japanese) landscape paintings reflect the Taoist belief in a unity with all life. This state of harmony could be achieved through the direct contemplation of nature. Artists were often scholars and philosophers who infused their landscape paintings with the mystical and transcendental spirit of the cosmos. By depicting mountains shrouded in mists and seemingly infinite spaces, artists such as Hsü Tao-ning (ca. 970–1052) expressed the majesty and vastness of nature. Although dwarfed by the setting, the figures of people are harmoniously integrated into the scene. The sublimity of Chinese landscapes was unmatched in Western art until the nineteenth century when mountains became popular subjects.

In the West, the influence of monotheistic religious doctrine discouraged landscape painting, and it suffered an eclipse of fourteen hundred years before reappearing during the late Middle Ages. The Catholic church forbid the worship of the gods and goddesses that had once personified the forces of nature. The biblical legend of God's banishment of Adam and Eve from the Garden of Eden further distanced human beings from the natural world (FIG. 14). In Giovanni di Paolo's (ca. 1403–1482) *Expulsion from Paradise* (1445), an archangel expels man and woman from a fertile grove of orange trees and wildflowers. Above them is the figure of God, omnipotent and enveloped in golden light, floating on the wings of angels. He points to their new home: a disc representing the Earth, barren, scarred by mountains, and sealed in celestial spheres and astrological signs of the zodiac. Although the artist faithfully translates the biblical text, he also depicts the beauty of nature through the careful observation of its details.

The Bible proclaimed man's divinely given dominion over the earth and was often used to justify nature's brutal exploitation.[21] The contemporary artist Paulette Nenner (1949–1988) interprets the schism between humans and nature that resulted from the influence of Christianity (FIG. 15). In her controversial sculpture *Crucified Coyote* (1981), the animal substitutes for the figure of Christ.[22] Wantonly killed by human beings who consider it a threat to cattle, the coyote is interpreted as a martyred figure.

By comparison to Western religions, Eastern beliefs appear to offer a more balanced view of the human relationship to nature. However, Chinese civilization engaged as much as did the Western world in deforestation and dramatic alterations to the landscape. In China, rice cultivation required the clearing of virgin forests and the practice of terracing denuded foothills. This pattern was repeated

13 • Hsü Tao-ning, detail from *Fishermen* (Yü-fu), ca. 1000

in India, despite the fact that Hinduism regards all life as sacred, and in Japan, even though Buddhism and Shintoism express similar ethical principles.

The daily interaction between people and the natural world, portrayed in Chinese landscape painting, makes a rare, early appearance in Ambrogio Lorenzetti's (1285–ca. 1348) fresco painting, *The Effects of Good Government in the City and the Country* (1337–39). In a detail from this work, the relationship between farming and wilderness and city and country is panoramically portrayed (FIG. 16). Using bird's-eye perspective, the artist documents the expansion of agriculture into the distant hills, which shield a few remaining forest groves. The painting also shows the close connection of city residents to the countryside, which offered fresh air and open space nearby. This symbiotic relationship would degenerate during and after the Industrial Revolution.

During the seventeenth century, landscape painting reemerged throughout Europe as a popular genre. Artists painted a variety of motifs — rocky outcrops, waterfalls, marshes, the sea — to influence mood, instill drama, and elevate thoughts. Although based on sketches from nature, landscape paintings were composed of imaginary views that became formularized. Claude Gelée, known as Claude Lorrain (1600–1682), and Nicolas Poussin (1594–1665) developed styles that

Man models himself after Earth.

Earth models itself after Heaven.

Heaven models itself after Tao.

And Tao models itself after Nature.

—*from* The Lao Tzu (Tao-te-ching)

14 • Giovanni di Paolo, *The Creation of the World and the Expulsion from Paradise* (predella panel), 1445

15 • Paulette Nenner, *Crucified Coyote*, 1982

were widely adapted by later generations of artists and influenced the direction of landscape painting. Their works offered an idealized and Arcadian vision of nature — timeless, ordered and free from strife — as a form of solace in an increasingly complex world. By contrast, the landscapes of Jacob van Ruisdael (1628/29–1682) reflected the earth's dynamic and changing aspects, providing a more realistic model of the world.

THE INDUSTRIAL REVOLUTION: THE CULMINATION OF LANDSCAPE PAINTING,
CITY SCENES AND INDUSTRIAL LANDSCAPES, IMAGES FROM THE DUST BOWL

The Industrial Revolution initiated a new, more insidious period of abuse and depletion of nature that continues unabated to this day. When coal was first mined to fuel the steam-generated engine — which was perfected by James Watt in 1769 — a degradation in the quality of life began. However, atmospheric pollution from the burning of hydrocarbons and water tainted by the effluents of industry were noted by residents and visitors to London as early as 1661, when John Evelyn (1620–1706), one of the founders of the Royal Society, wrote a treatise on air pollution. According to Evelyn, pulmonary problems accounted for 50 percent of the

16 • Ambrogio Lorenzetti, *Effects of Good Government in the City and Country* (detail from scenes in the countryside), 1337–39

deaths in London. Such consequences of environmental degeneration sharpened the contrast between the city and countryside. Agriculture was also affected as steam-powered machines replaced human labor and propelled the cultivation of ever-larger tracts of land. Deforestation accelerated, and populations continued to explode as rural residents were forced to relocate to expanding cities, which now housed factories.

These environmental changes mirrored an entirely new philosophy that substituted an organic conception of nature, based on agricultural societies' dependence on the rhythms of the seasons, with a mechanistic one, based on the new machines that propelled early capitalism and industrialization. Reflecting a growing distance from nature, this new philosophy defined God and the cosmos through analogy to a giant clock, autonomous and anonymous.[23]

Many artists and literary figures rejected this mechanical view of the universe. The Romantic school of literature emerged as poets like Lord Byron (1788–1824) and William Blake (1757–1827) steeped their writings in a rapturous reverence for nature. In Europe and the United States, artists responded by painting the wonders of nature that they discovered while exploring all corners of the earth. By joining navigational explorations and survey teams, they were able to paint every type of terrain on all continents, including Antarctica. They documented unusual topographies and exotic lands through drawings that later became the foundation for large-scale paintings completed in the studio. Their work reflected a new interest in the natural sciences, which flourished during this time. Landscape artists observed the intricate workings of nature in the same spirit that sparked new discoveries in geology, geography, and biology. Although motivated to capture the reality of site, artists experienced and romantically interpreted its transcendental aspect, and viewers were able to lose themselves in nature's mystery and drama.

To see the world in a grain of sand,

And a heaven in a wild flower;

Hold infinity in the palm of your hand

And eternity in an hour.

—William Blake

(*from* Songs of Innocence, *1801–3*)

17 • Frederic Edwin Church, *La Magdalena (Scene on the Magdalena)*, 1854

I live not in myself, but I become

Portion of that around me; and to me

High mountains are a feeling, but the hum

Of human cities torture . . .

—Lord Byron

(from Child Harold's Pilgrimage, *1816)*

During the nineteenth century, landscape painting reached its apogee in Europe and the United States. At no other time in Western history had nature stimulated so many artists and varieties of subjects.

Mountains, symbols of wilderness and once considered by Christian theologians as too dismal and ungodly a setting for human beings, inspired some of the greatest works of nineteenth-century Romantic art by Joseph Mallord William Turner (1775–1851), Caspar David Friedrich (1774–1840), and Frederic Edwin Church (1826–1900), among others. Landscape paintings of the Alps, Scandinavia, the Rockies, and the Andes encouraged tourism to these regions. Artists often made topographical sketches that were later engraved and colored and then published in travel guides. So began the age of the travelogue and the pinnacle of the sublime in art. All of these works interpreted nature's majesty and awesome character. Through art and travel, people rediscovered the sacred in nature.

Artists like Frederic Edwin Church, Martin Johnson Heade (1819–1904), and François-Auguste Biard journeyed to South America and recognized the importance of the rain forest as a vast encyclopedia of knowledge and a source of beauty long before the current public concern for its preservation (FIG. 17). Despite the hardships of intense heat and mosquitoes, they penetrated into the primeval jungle to sketch and describe exotic plants, fauna, and indigenous tribes. For them, it was still an unknown world that offered challenging, new information to present to the public. All of these artists were inspired by the great naturalist-explorer, Alexander von Humboldt (1769–1859), who traveled through Central and South America for five years and wrote an influential compendium of natural history titled *Cosmos* (5 vols., 1845–62). Here Humboldt described the harmonies existing within the complexities of nature and pronounced the limitless opportunities that the tropics offered artists both as a visual resource and for spiritual enlightenment. In Church's *La Magdalena (Scene on the Magdalena)* (1854), the naturalistic details of vegetation and a vast panorama, encompassing mountains, rivers, and virgin forests, are bathed in the light of divinity. For the artist, South America was the quintessence of God's creation in its magnificent abundance of life and its varied topography.

Not only was nature admired for her awesome and majestic spectacles but also for the places that offered serenity and solitude. Artists like Theodore Rousseau (1812–1867), who painted outside Paris in the forest of Fountainebleau, discovered the "voice of the trees" in nature's more intimate enclaves. Here he experienced nature's spiritual essence. The desire for a more direct contact with the earth led Rousseau and other artists to paint extensively outdoors in oil for the first time in the history of the landscape tradition. This revolutionary method inspired the movement that came to be called Impressionism.

Although many artists were alarmed at the rapid rate of deforestation and urban growth, they seldom communicated this through their paintings. Instead, they responded by expressing a renewed reverence for nature. Their landscapes preserved for the future those sites in nature that were rapidly disappearing.

In the United States, Thomas Cole (1801–1848), the founder of the Hudson River School of landscape painting, did express his concern for the state of nature and the cities in a series of five paintings titled *The Course of Empire* (1834–36). In the first three works, Cole depicts the evolution of society from hunting-and-gathering (*The Savage State*) to pastoralism (*The Arcadian State*) and culminating in an imperial civilization (*The Consummation of Empire*). The fourth painting, *Destruction*, represents the devastation of civilization and the annihilation of an entire city populace (FIG. 18). In the final painting, titled *Desolation*, all that remains of a once grand city is a classical architectural column, supporting not a great building but a heron's nest (FIG. 19). All of the structures are now ruins overgrown with vegetation, and nature reclaims mastery over its domain. These paintings, like the ones similar in theme by the English artist John Martin (1789–1854), may reflect the influence of Thomas Malthus (1766–1834), who first offered a serious warning of overpopulation. Even if Cole was not responding directly to Malthus's famous treatise, *An Essay on the Principle of Population* (1798), *The Course of Empire* allegorically alludes to the belief that "progress" may not be in the best interests of humanity.

As the ravage of nature continued, a new, more organic philosophy developed to counter materialism and the mechanistic view of the world. Transcen-

18 • Thomas Cole, *Course of Empire: Destruction*, 1836

19 • Thomas Cole, *Course of Empire: Desolation*, 1836

20 • Sanford Gifford, *Hunter Mountain, Twilight,* 1866

dentalism, originating in New England during the mid-nineteenth century, was a literary as well as philosophical movement that expressed faith in the divinity of nature. Ralph Waldo Emerson (1803–1882) and Henry David Thoreau (1817–1862), two of America's most important writers, professed the belief that nature was imbued with a spirit embracing and connecting all living things.

In *Walden* (1854), Thoreau contemplated his life in the woods by Walden Pond and asked, "Shall I not have intelligence with the earth? Am I not partly leaves and vegetable mound myself?" This statement expressed a revolutionary concept that would become one of the foundations of environmental ethics. Thoreau's ideas bear Eastern religious overtones, and the author acknowledged the influence of the Hindu religion. East and West met again a century later when Mohandas K. Gandhi (1869–1948) paid homage to Thoreau as he advocated *Ahimsa,* the belief that change can be initiated by nonviolence.

Transcendentalism may have fostered an atmosphere that encouraged artists to respond more directly to the destruction of nature by incorporating into their compositions one very important landscape motif, the tree stump (FIG. 20). As early as the 1840s, Thomas Cole, and later Sanford Robinson Gifford (1823–1880), along with other artists, transformed the image of the sacred tree that was introduced in ancient art. During earlier periods of deforestation, the artist used the tree to affirm nature's life-generating power. Now, the tree's symbolism was changed to connote the desecration of nature through human intervention.[24] Felled trees and

21 • Roger Brown, *Lewis and Clark Trail*, 1979

their remaining trunks were stark reminders of what once was considered the American continent's equivalent to the cathedrals of Europe. The destruction of the sacred tree — sacrificed to economic progress — was also noted in poems, including those of Thomas Cole and, later, Walt Whitman.

The dramatic demarcation and contrast between wilderness and human settlement is the subject of Sanford Robinson Gifford's *Hunter Mountain, Twilight* (1866) (FIG. 20). The artist's unusual composition draws the viewer immediately to the tree stumps, ruins in a field where cattle now graze. A farmhouse is nestled in a small remnant of woods for protection. In the distance, a panoramic view of the valley shows it almost completely cleared of forest. Rising smoke indicates the

Our village life would stagnate if it were not for the unexplored forests and meadows which surround it. We need the tonic of wildness . . . At the same time that we earnest to explore and learn all things, we require that all things be mysterious and unexplorable, that land and sea be infinitely wild, unsurveyed and unfathomed by us because unfathomable. We can never have enough of nature.

—*Henry David Thoreau*

(*from* Walden, *1854*)

22 • Albert Bierstadt, *The Last of the Buffalo*, 1888

presence of more farms. Nature could still inspire awe and Gifford communicated its transcendental powers through the golden rays of light. The twilight effect bestows a note of melancholy on the scene, as the artist poignantly refers to the demise of the vast expanse of virgin forests that once dominated the continent.

The image of the tree stump is later used by Winslow Homer (1836–1910) to express a similar ravaged state of nature. The artist, who lived in isolation along the rocky coastline of Maine and made frequent trips to the Adirondacks, understood and portrayed nature's sublime forces. In *Huntsman and Dogs* (1891, Philadelphia Museum of Art) deforestation is dramatized by a close-up view of a single tree trunk that dominates the entire composition. A trapper, dependent upon the woods for survival, sees in the stump a premonition of his own passing.

Deforestation is once again an issue that has captured the attention of contemporary artists alarmed by clear-cutting techniques that decimate vestiges of virgin lands worldwide. In *Lewis and Clark Trail* (1979), Roger Brown updates the iconography of the tree stump (FIG. 21). He lampoons clear-cutting by depicting a repetitive spiraling composition of dead stumps ascending a mountain slope. Through abstraction and a tilted perspective, the composition assumes the shape of a machine similar to a chain saw. By placing three real tree stumps on a shelf in front of the painting, Brown's message is made more concrete.

The assault on virgin trees began in the nineteenth century, propelled by the railroad, which appeared in many landscape paintings as a symbol of the speed of industrialization and the opening of the American West to development and exploitation. The period also witnessed a total disregard for human life, which resulted in the displacement of Native Americans into reservations and the annihilation of them and their culture.

Artists like George Catlin (1796–1872), recognizing that Manifest Destiny and "progress" were causing the destruction of nature and native populations, devoted their entire careers to systematically documenting indigenous peoples. One of the most important works to portray the extinction of both the Native American and the buffalo is *The Last of the Buffalo* (1888) (FIG. 22) by Albert Bierstadt (1830–1902). Instead of depicting the loss of the bison, the artist celebrates its former glorious dominance over the Plains. The animals stretch endlessly across the landscape, and the native peoples, whose culture depended upon the species for survival, are engaged in the hunt. *The Last of the Buffalo* is a glimpse into the past, an attempt to preserve for history a record of nature and life that Bierstadt experienced as a participant in Frederick W. Lander's survey expedition in 1859. However, as early as 1832, Catlin prophesied their extinction and proposed the country's first national park as a reserve for both Native Americans and the buffalo.

As forests were hacked away and entire species wiped out, artists like Bierstadt and Thomas Moran (1837–1926) escaped to areas of the continent still untouched by pioneers. Here they painted Yosemite Valley and Yellowstone, landscapes that appeared beyond man's control (FIG. 23). Viewing their paintings, people were able to transcend the harsh realities of change and progress. Many who admired and collected these works — railroad barons and industrialists — were those same people who engaged in nature's destruction. Landscape painting promoted the illusion that they lived in harmony with nature.

The majority of Western landscape paintings dating from the second half of the nineteenth century ignored the realities of conquest and exploitation of nature that were intrinsic to the success of Manifest Destiny.[25] Many of the artists welcomed the arrival of the railroad, since it gave them access to the natural wonders of the continent. However, it is unlikely that artists intended to communicate and contribute to a spirit of expansionism through their work. While political leaders, industrialists, and segments of the public may themselves have viewed these works as celebrating the conquest of nature, these same landscapes acted as catalysts for its preservation. Landscape painters and photographers who returned East with awesome views influenced the formation of national parks. And although the motivation for establishing these parks was, for many, primarily aesthetic rather than ecological, it was a first attempt to protect natural resources from the grips of development.

Yosemite Valley, the world's first nature preserve, was set aside as a state park in 1864, after the great groves of redwoods and sequoias were felled in California. The establishment of Yellowstone National Park followed in 1872, the year that Moran painted the *Grand Canyon of the Yellowstone*, which was purchased for a princely sum of $10,000 by the federal government (FIG. 23). In this painting, the artist and his fellow explorers are reduced to insignificance by the eroded cliffs and giant trees. Two men, standing on the edge of a precipice, gaze across a vast chasm to a distant waterfall. Moran's elevated perspective provides the viewer with an even

It is a melancholy contemplation for one who has travelled as I have, through these realms, and seen this noble animal in all its pride and glory, to contemplate it so rapidly wasting from the world, drawing the irresistible conclusion . . . that its species is soon to be extinguished . . .

What a beautiful and thrilling specimen for America to preserve and hold up to the view of her refined citizens and the world, in future ages! A *nation's Park*, containing man and beast, in all the wild and freshness of their nature's beauty!

—*George Catlin (from* North American Indians . . . *1832–39)*

23 • Thomas Moran, *Grand Canyon of the Yellowstone*, 1872

greater panorama, which includes the Rocky Mountains and the steam of erupting geysers. Although not nearly large enough to accommodate the vast numbers of people who visit today, these national parks were essential components of an early conservation effort. It is true that economic considerations of tourism were partly responsible for their establishment, but so also were the efforts of such people as John Muir (1838–1914), naturalist and founder of the Sierra Club, who believed in the importance of wilderness for its own sake and devoted his life to preserving the Sierra Mountains.

It is not surprising that the National Parks movement was initiated by Easterners who lived in big cities. People like Frederick Law Olmsted (1822–1903), landscape architect of New York City's Central Park and one of the first advocates of wilderness preservation, directly experienced the urban problems of overpopulation and shrinking open space for recreation. Lobbying for city parks subsequently became part of a growing civic movement and influenced the design of every major city in the United States. New York's Central Park is one of the masterpieces of urban planning (FIG. 24). As early as 1844, the poet, newspaper editor, and close friend of Thomas Cole, William Cullen Bryant (1794–1878), wrote several editorials in *The Evening Post* advocating a great park in the heart of New York City.[26] However, it was not until 1857 that public officials appropriated money and designated Olmsted as the landscape architect.

24 • *Central Park, Huddlestone Arch,* prior to 1900

Olmsted firmly believed in the importance of open spaces where a growing population could breathe fresh air, find escape from the sweltering summer heat, and experience the spiritual enlightenment afforded by natural scenery. In 1858, he described the aims and motivations that shaped his design for Central Park:

> Two classes of improvements were to be planned for this purpose; one directed to secure pure and wholesome air, to act through the lungs; the other to secure an antithesis of objects of vision to those of the streets and houses, which should act remedially by impressions on the mind and suggestions to the imagination.

25 • Jacob Riis, *"Five Cents a Spot" — Lodgers in a crowded Bayard Street Tenement*, ca. 1889

It is one great purpose of the Park to supply to the hundreds of thousands of tired workers, who have no opportunity to spend their summers in the country, a specimen of God's handiwork that shall be to them, inexpensively, what a month or two in the White Mountains or the Adirondacks is, at great cost, to those in easier circumstances. The time will come when New York will be built up, when all the grading and filling will be done, and when the picturesquely varied, rocky formations of the Island will have been converted into formations for rows of monotonous straight streets, and piles of erect buildings. There will be no suggestion left of its present varied surface, with the single exception of the few acres contained in the Park.[27]

Although influenced by the picturesque and pastoral design of English landscaping so popular at the time, Olmsted did want to maintain the rural look and feel of the city's topography. This concept contrasted with more conventional city gardens, promenades, and public squares, which are designed to assert the urbanity of the city.[28] He took advantage of the rusticity of the site by incorporating existing glacial rock outcrops into his design and using rough-hewn stones for bridges. The flow of water — lakes, streams, waterfalls — is a major component of the design, which heightens the natural effect. To this day, there are sections of Central Park that convey the atmosphere of the countryside. Olmstead and his Central Park influenced the City Beautiful Movement, a campaign initiated by leaders in the arts and business at the turn of the century to make cities cleaner and more livable through political reform and enlightened urban planning.[29]

Although the deteriorating quality of city life inspired the creation of Central Park, it was not until the end of the century that the squalor in which the majority of people lived was publicly exposed (FIG. 25). In 1890, public attention was focused on the condition of life in New York City's Lower East Side by an influential book, *How the Other Half Lives*, written and photographed by Jacob August Riis (1849–1914). Riis, who began his career as a police reporter for the *New York Tribune*, accompanied health officials inspecting for overcrowded housing conditions. For five cents, people often slept in bunks and on the floor of small rooms with up to twelve men and women. The photograph titled *Five Cents a Spot*, taken with a flashlight in the middle of the night, was one of a hundred that documented the environment of newly arrived immigrants. With these photographs, Riis spearheaded a reform movement that included the passage of sanitary housing regulations and the construction of more parks and playgrounds.

A relatively recent art medium — invented only in 1839 — photography quickly became a powerful force for rallying public opinion and effecting change. The success of Riis's work inspired a generation of younger artists who consider him the father of photojournalism. Through its immediacy and sense of urgency, photojournalism aims to shock the public by exposing human and environmental problems. The work of Dorothea Lange (1895–1965) and Arthur Rothstein (b. 1915), portraying the environmental catastrophe known as the Dust Bowl, and W. Eugene Smith (1918–1978), who documented the devastating effects of mercury poisoning on the life of the people and bay at Minamata, Japan, communicate the suffering of victims of environmental abuse (FIGS. 29, 30, 33).

Not long after Riis published *How the Other Half Lives*, artists began to portray the street life of the city. Their works were not enthusiastically received by art collectors, critics, or institutions because they threatened the status quo defined by academic art traditions and wealthy patrons. Until the turn of the century, artists depicted the life-style of the city's upper class — their tea parties, balls, croquet games — in an exquisitely polished style. It was not until the early 1900s that a group of artists, derogatorily named the Ashcan School for the subjects they portrayed, began focusing on the other realities of the urban environment (FIG. 26). In *Cliff Dwellers* (1913), George Bellows (1882–1925) paints a typical New York City neighborhood of closely spaced tenements. It is a steamy summer day, and people crowd into the narrow streets shared by trolley cars, carts, and vendors. There are people everywhere, hanging out of windows

26 • George Wesley Bellows, *Cliff Dwellers*, 1913

and sitting on balconies, stoops, and even the street. Using loose, expressionistic brush strokes, Bellows portrays his subject with dignity and vitality. He does not define individual personalities but seeks to capture the throng of humanity. The artist, who also illustrated articles for the socialist magazine *The Masses*, sympathized with those people who were forced by poverty to live on overcrowded, treeless streets without the means of escape enjoyed by wealthy New Yorkers.

In addition to overpopulation and the disappearance of open space, the industrial city was transformed by the introduction of the factory. During the Roaring Twenties, machines and industry seized the artist's imagination. Great wealth was generated, and many American artists depicted the power and glory of expanding technology. Most of these paintings were based on a chauvinistic pride in the industrial accomplishments of the United States. In their search for an intrinsically modern American style, which would liberate them aesthetically from the dominating influence of Europe, artists painted the skyscrapers, power plants, and factories located in or near major cities. While these artists celebrated industrial-

27 • Charles Sheeler, *American Landscape*, 1930

And did the Countenance Divine

Shine forth upon our clouded hills?

And was Jerusalem builded here

Among these dark Satanic Mills?

—*William Blake (from* Milton, *1804–8)*

ism, many in developing countries like Mexico clearly questioned its effects on human life (FIGS. 27, 28).

By its very title, *American Landscape* (1930), a view of the Ford automobile factory in River Rouge, Michigan, Charles Sheeler (1883–1965) asserts the supremacy of the new industrial scenery. Until this time, landscapes had been composed of trees, mountains, and other natural features, which were important sources of spiritual enlightenment. In *American Landscape*, Sheeler implies that the power of religion, once associated with pantheistic nature, has now been conferred upon technology. A sense of eternity is evoked by the uncanny tranquillity and order of the scene. Pristinely composed, the painting is dominated by white, which sanitizes even the pollution from a smokestack.

American artists like Sheeler largely ignored the negative effects of industrialization. One has only to compare the Mexican artist David Alfaro Siqueiros's (1896–1974) *Echo of a Scream* (1937) to Sheeler's painting to find an alternative interpretation of industrial development. Sitting amidst the metal debris of what looks like a war-torn wasteland, a young boy cries aloud. His pain is dramatically visu-

28 • David Alfaro Siqueiros, *Echo of a Scream*, 1937

alized by a giant head, identical to his own, hauntingly suspended in space. In the far distance, the artist includes a view of storage tanks that suggest the new urban fortress, as well as a lone, sacred tree, symbolizing the loss of nature. Siqueiros recognized that industrialization was not necessarily synonymous with progress nor a panacea for poverty. By moving to the city in order to find employment in factories, people often experienced a sense of rootlessness and loss of individual identity. This alienation is powerfully represented in *Echo of a Scream.*

Sheeler and many other American artists depicted a utopian industrial dream devoid of flesh and blood. Popularized during the Thirties, these scenes rarely acknowledged the squalid condition of factory workers, which was documented by photojournalists like Lewis Hine (1874–1940), who photographed children in

The maintenance of the regional setting, the green matrix, is essential for the culture of cities. Where this setting has been defaced, despoiled or obliterated, the deterioration of the city must follow, for the relationship is symbiotic.

—*Lewis Mumford*

(*from* The City in History, *1961*)

29 • Dorothea Lange, from *An American Exodus: A Record of Human Erosion in the Thirties,* 1939

sweatshops, coal mines, and factories in the eastern United States. In reality, the industrial cities of the United States were deteriorating and so was the countryside.

Although artists like Grant Wood (1892–1945) and John Steuart Curry (1897–1946) painted bucolic scenes of bountiful harvests, something sinister was happening to the land. The Plains were experiencing one of the worst ecological disasters ever instigated by man. From 1930 through 1941, eroding land and dust storms that circulated as far north as Chicago plagued farmers in Oklahoma, Texas, New Mexico, and Kansas. Although lack of rainfall was partly to blame for this environmental disaster, the farmers who overcultivated the land were largely responsible. By deep plowing and farming every spare acre, they stripped the earth of the natural vegetation that had held the soil in place.[30]

The year of greatest damage was 1938, when over 23 million acres were depleted of two-and-a-half to five inches of topsoil. Statistics are mind boggling, but they do little to suggest the extent of tragedy. Only the photographs and paintings that

30 • Arthur Rothstein, *Dust Storm, Cimarron County, Oklahoma,* 1936

remain portray the trauma to people and the land (FIGS. 29–31). Photographers, sponsored by the Farm Security Administration (FSA), documented the condition of migrant workers and the environment in the southern Plains states, referred to by a news journalist as the Dust Bowl. Were it not for artists like Alexander Hogue (b. 1898), Joe Jones (1909–1963), Dorothea Lange (1895–1965), Walker Evans (1903–1975), Russell Lee (b. 1903), and Arthur Rothstein (b. 1915), as well as writers like John Steinbeck (1902–1968) whose *Grapes of Wrath* (1939) is still widely read (and even better known through the film), the Dust Bowl would have been forgotten by the public.

When the Farm Security Administration commissioned photographers Dorothea Lange and Arthur Rothstein to document the environmental and human conditions in the Plains, they were not intentionally promoting art or artists. Instead, the bureau was instituted by Franklin Roosevelt's administration to garner support for New Deal economic measures that included aid to the farm belt. Nevertheless, the photographer's imagery transcends mere documentation and political propaganda. Their works are marked by the drama and urgency of the artist's emotional response and first-hand observation. Lange represents a stark landscape that stretches into an endless vista of shifting sands (FIG. 29). The human presence is a mere echo of a previous life now abandoned. In *Dust Storm, Cimmaron County* (1936), Rothstein provides a rare glimpse of a man and his two sons as they run for shelter in a battered and partially buried building (FIG. 30). The powerful emotions evoked by this photograph derive, in part, from what is missing; earth and sky are indistinguishable from each other as the dust blankets an empty environment.

Dried by years of drought and pulverized by machine-drawn gang disc plows, the soil was literally thrown to the winds. . . . The winds churned the soil, leaving vast stretches of farms blown and hummocked. . . . They loosened the hold of the settlers on the land, and like particles of dust drove them rolling down ribbons of highway.

—*Dorothea Lange and*

Paul Schuster Taylor

(*from* An American Exodus:

A Record of Human Erosion in

the Thirties, *1939)*

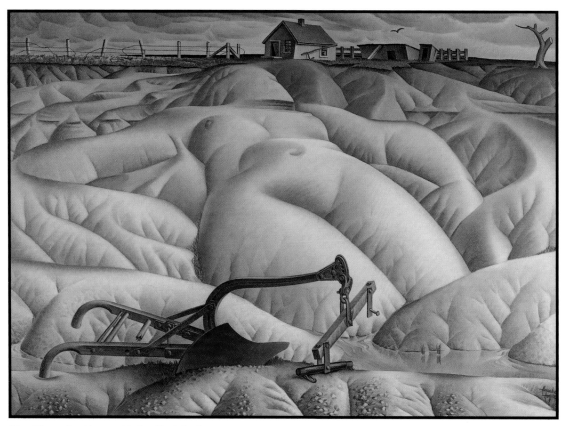

31 • Alexander Hogue, *Mother Earth Laid Bare*, 1938

The Great Plains are normally semidesert with conditions that make it difficult to farm. Originally, the area was covered with a variety of grasses that preserved the soil and supported bison, antelope, and other animals. The Comanche supported themselves in a sound ecological manner by deliberately regulating their population and adapting to the natural cycles of fertility and drought, which come and go approximately every twenty years.

The farmers who arrived from the East developed a new method called "dry farming" that could be implemented with little water. It encouraged deep ploughing and, later, investments in tractors to turn under the grasses that held the soil in place. This intensification of agriculture helped to reap more profits, which in turn caused even more available land to be so cultivated. The earth soon became vulnerable to the winds of drought.

In Alexander Hogue's painting, *Mother Earth Laid Bare* (1938), the implement responsible for the Dust Bowl — the plow — is isolated in the foreground (FIG. 31). The scorched landscape beyond discretely assumes the sensual shape of a reclining nude woman. By melding her contours with those of the earth, Hogue refers to the ancient beliefs surrounding the worship of the nurturing Great Goddess. The artist warns that the abuse of nature results in severing our connection to life. On the horizon, the deserted farm and the single, lifeless tree are evidence of human disregard for the earth.

Almost fifty years later, Ana Mendietta (1949–1985) similarly suggests the close association between the earth and woman and the often violent abuses they both suffer (FIG. 32). In *Birth (Nacimiento)* (1982), the artist traced her own figure in the mud and shaped it into a vessel for gunpowder. During the process of lighting the explosives and watching the fire burn into the earth, the artist engaged in a ritualistic act that served as both a personal cathartic experience and a socio-political statement about the rape of woman and nature. However, the title implies a hopeful message: From the ashes emerges the renewal of life.

The tragedy of the Dust Bowl was soon forgotten as World War II drew to a close and the United States experienced a business boom that propelled the most intensive years of industrialization. The extraordinary growth of the agriculture, timber, plastics, and chemical industries created a gap by which we further distanced ourselves from nature. Everything that was once made from natural materials and was thus recyclable and degradable was replaced by synthetics, requiring huge expenditures of energy (in the form of nonrenewable fossil fuels) to produce.

The residue of the processes of production left a toxic wake of mercury, PCBs, benzenes, and heavy metals that entered streams and landfills to contaminate water supplies. Overjoyed that the economy was moving again after the years of the Great Depression, most people, including artists, barely noticed.

During the 1950s, a group of artists known as the Abstract Expressionists responded to the existential crisis of humanity, precipitated by the horrors of World War II and the atomic bomb, rather than to environmental issues. Artists like Adolph Gottlieb (1903–1974), Barnett Newman (1905–1970), and Jackson Pollock (1912–1956) interpreted the mythic images of preindustrial peoples, notably Native Americans, to express universal themes of creation and destruction. They were also concerned with formal issues of style that enabled them to develop a vocabulary distinct from that of European art.

The next major movement in art — Pop — focused on the objects of mass consumption popularized by the media. Artists like James Rosenquist (b. 1933) and Andy Warhol (1928–1987) did not engage the subject of environmentalism but rather celebrated society's affluence and absorption with products. Through paintings, collages, sculptures, and prints of cigarettes, beer, Wonderbread, and Coca Cola, artists depicted the trappings of mid-twentieth-century life without criticism or social commentary. Their emphasis on the object was also a means to forge a new identity for art that had earlier been dominated by abstraction.

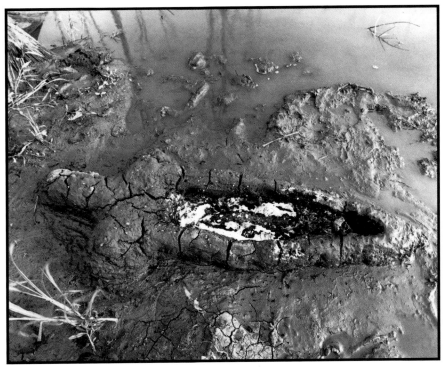

32 • Ana Mendieta, *Birth (Nacimiento)*, 1982

One woman, a solo voice amid this din of commerce, sounded an alarm that would effect a new awareness of nature's fragility and initiate the modern environmental movement. In 1962, Rachel Carson (1907–1964), a marine biologist, published a stirring and factual account of the effects of synthetic pesticides on life. In *Silent Spring*, Carson described the death of wildlife and the destruction of their habitat as a result of agricultural pesticides. Although she concentrated on DDT, her discourse extended to the harmful effects of all chemicals:

The contamination of our world is not alone a matter of mass spraying. Indeed, for most of us, this is of less importance than the innumerable small-scale exposures to which we are subjected day to day, year after year. Like the constant dripping of water that in turn wears away the hardest stone, this birth-to-death contact with dangerous chemicals may in the end prove disastrous. Each of these recurrent exposures, no matter how slight, contributes to the progressive buildup of chemicals in our bodies and so to cumulative poisoning. Probably no person is immune to contact with this spreading contamination unless he lives in the most isolated situation imaginable. Lulled by the soft sell and the hidden persuader, the average citizen is seldom aware of the deadly materials with which he is surrounding himself; indeed, he may not realize he is using them at all.[31]

33 • W. Eugene Smith, *Tomoko Uemura in her Bath,* 1972, from the series *Minamata, Japan 1971–75*

Although the chemical companies launched a campaign to discredit Carson, *Silent Spring* influenced political and public opinion. DDT was finally banned from United States farmlands, although it continues to be produced and exported overseas to developing countries like India. The dependency on synthetic chemicals that poison insects, as well as other creatures, continues unabated to this day.

Throughout the 1960s, a period of great social and political activism, environmental concern mounted. Public pressure forced the passage of important pieces of regulatory legislation, including the Clean Air Act (1963). Lawyers banded together to establish the Environmental Defense Fund (1967), and Greenpeace was founded (1969). In 1968, television viewers were awed by the beauty and fragility of the first view of Earth from space, beamed down from Apollo VIII. The decade culminated in the first Earth Day celebration (1970), which witnessed millions of people expressing their concern for the fate of the planet.

This new environmental consciousness would be further ignited by the publication of an important book by W. Eugene and Aileen M. Smith, conceived in the tradition of Riis's *How the Other Half Lives.* His photographs and commentary in *Minamata* (1975) alerted people around the world to the tragic consequences of mercury poisoning in Minamata Bay, Japan (FIG. 33). Chisso, a chemical company located in Minamata, had been discharging its toxic waste into the bay for over twenty years. Beginning in the 1950s, the marine life and people of the region began to be contaminated. Despite the death of over one thousand people, and protests to halt the environmental abuse, dumping continued until 1969, when a court order forced the company to accept blame for the disaster. Smith and his wife, Aileen, lived in Minamata for three years in order to experience the tragedy first-hand, photographing the bay, factory, fishing fleets, and people who suffered from the degenerative nervous system disease that directly results from ingesting mercury. These photographs helped focus public attention on the issue of water pollution. Symbolic of irresponsible industrial environmental policies, they continue to shock and alert people to the necessity of civic action and vigilance over nature and human life. They foreshadow the more recent environmental disasters that have occurred in Bhopol, India and Chernobyl, Russia.

•

People have always altered their environment, often creating damaging and stressful conditions that jeopardize their own survival. Early artists responded by introducing new imagery and genres that celebrated nature's powers of growth, decay, and renewal. In hunting-and-gathering and agricultural societies, art and ritual reflected the symbiotic relationship between people and the land. Understanding of this connection was subsequently lost, especially during the Industrial Revolution, and the flourishing of landscape painting represents a direct response to this schism. Like their preindustrial forebears, landscape painters communicated the spiritual and physical energies of the earth.

During the nineteenth and twentieth centuries, a few artists referred, for the first time, to the exploitation of nature. Artists also began addressing problems in the urban environment — overpopulation and the loss of open space. Photojournalism, emerging at the end of the nineteenth century and expanding its scope during the twentieth, contributed to public environmental awareness of deleterious conditions in both the city and the countryside.

Through the twentieth century, many artists continued to express the spirituality of nature through landscape painting. Artists who were more abstractly oriented — Arthur G. Dove (1880–1946), Georgia O'Keeffe (1887–1985), Charles Burchfield (1893–1967), Mark Tobey (1890–1976) — and those who realistically depicted the landscape — Andrew Wyeth (b. 1917) and Neil Welliver (b. 1929) — continued the tradition of nineteenth-century artists who preserved nature.

By contrast, only a few contemporary artists attempted to convey the damaging consequences of the widening gap between people and the natural world. This changed in the 1960s as artists responded to a growing environmental awareness by interpreting nature in radically new ways. This movement, known as "environmental art," is having a profound effect upon both art and nature.

Pollution growth is still running far

ahead of any anti-pollution

conscience. But what we also found

in Minamata was the kind of courage

and stubborness that can encourage

other threatened people not only to

refuse to give in, but also to work at

righting their own situations.

—W. Eugene and Aileen M. Smith

(from Minamata, 1975)

2

Environmental Art:

New Approaches to Nature

THE POLITICAL AND SOCIAL CLIMATE DURING THE 1960s encouraged a fresh approach to both art and nature. As an increasing number of people began to question traditional values and governmental policies regarding Vietnam, racial segregation, women's status, and the environment, many artists began their own soul-searching. By examining art's relationship to society and the conventional materials and media of their profession, a group of artists in the United States and Europe started to challenge established assumptions about making and exhibiting art. Many turned to nature and began interpreting its life-generating forces to create radically new kinds of art. This movement became known as "environmental art."

Environmental art encompasses a variety of forms that reflect a wide range of approaches to nature. It includes permanent sculptures like the *Spiral Jetty* (1970) by Robert Smithson (1938–1973) (FIG. 34). Labeled "earth art" or "earthworks," they are created *in* the landscape and built with the indigenous materials of the site. By contrast, the movement also includes the temporary site-specific sculptures of Christo, who places manufactured materials *on* the landscape in such works as *The Running Fence, Sonoma and Marin Counties, California* (1972–76) (FIG. 35). Environmental art also refers to indoor gallery installations in which the artist transforms the space into a field of growth, as in Helen Mayer Harrison's and Newton Harrison's *Survival Piece #5: Portable Orchard* (1972) (FIG. 43). Along with plant

34 • Robert Smithson, *Spiral Jetty*, April 1970

35 • Christo, *Running Fence, Sonoma and Marin Counties, California,* 1972–76

life as art, environmental art can include animals as art, as exemplified by Joseph Beuys's *Coyote. I Like America and America Likes Me* (1974), a performance with a live coyote that dramatized the connection between human beings and other animals (FIG. 48). The movement also encompasses works that use elements of nature to interpret specific ecological problems, as did Hans Haacke's *Rhinewater Purification Plant* (1972) (FIG. 39), and outdoor ecological artworks that introduce flora and fauna into the city, as in *Time Landscape: Greenwich Village, New York* by Alan Sonfist (planted 1978) (FIG. 70) and Bonnie Sherk's *Crossroads Community/The Farm* (1974–1980) (FIGS. 49–51).

Defining specific tendencies within environmental art sometimes obscures the fact that many works are richly layered, and artists often move freely from one area to another and from indoor to outdoor work. For instance, Sonfist has responded to nature's diversity by creating a similarly versatile body of work that includes isolating natural mineral crystals whose patterns reflect changes in light and temperature (1966–72) (FIG. 36), extracting cores of earth and bedrock from a variety of sites in Manhattan (1972), and addressing the environmental issue of air pollution by taking air samples at various locations and posting the results on the spot (1969). Such works demonstrate the overlap of ideas within the oeuvre of an individual artist and the environmental art movement as a whole.

Of the many artists who create environmental art, only those bearing a direct relationship to the evolution of ecological art will be discussed in this volume. Many artworks indirectly relate to ecology by respecting nature and establishing a reverent relationship between the viewer and the earth. For instance, Michael Singer makes ephemeral sculpture from natural materials like bamboo, which eventually fade back into the landscape where they are recycled. Richard Long and Hamish Fulton journey across the land and use photography to suggest the qual-

... Now, however, it is no longer regarded as romantic but exceedingly realistic to fight for every tree, every plot of undeveloped land, every stream as yet unpoisoned, every old town center, and against every thoughtless reconstruction scheme. And it is no longer considered romantic to speak of nature. . . .

— *Joseph Beuys*

(from Manifesto *on the foundation of a "Free International School for Creativity and Interdisciplinary Research")*

36 • Alan Sonfist, *Crystal Monument*, 1966–1972

ity of their experience. These works sensitize the viewer to nature's fragility and the vastness of its domain.

Environmental art relates to two other important American movements — minimal and process art — that emerged during the 1960s. Both were concerned with extending traditional boundaries of form, space, and materials. Minimalist artists like Tony Smith (1912–1980) created large, geometric sculptures made from industrial materials whose overwhelming presence in the art gallery demanded more space. To artists such as Robert Morris and Robert Smithson, who both began their careers as minimalists, earthworks were a logical extension of their earlier interests. Nature provided an opportunity for them to translate primary, abstract forms on a large scale.

In contrast to the commercially fabricated materials used to create hard-edge minimal sculpture, process art was defined by nonrigid materials — rope, fabric, lead — that could be scattered, thrown, or poured. The subject of the work was the process itself, which expressed the changeable aspects of the material and its potential to expand endlessly in all directions. One of the most dramatic works that defined the artist's concern for process was Richard Serra's *Splash* pieces (1968), created by throwing molten lead into the space between the wall and floor mouldings. In process art, the compositions were often determined by chance and the nature of the material. By allowing nature itself to determine the form and content of the work, environmental artists share many of the concerns defined by process art.

Environmental art was important not only because it offered a new way of creating art and thinking about it, but also because it called attention to nature. Not since the nineteenth century have so many artists interpreted the natural world with such intensity. Unlike earlier painters who depicted specific landscape features, environmental artists visualize the forces, processes, and phenomena of nature: organic growth (FIG. 37), light (FIG. 73), water (FIG. 39), crystals (FIG. 36), and other elements. Nature was no longer captured in an eternal moment through static paintings but interpreted as alive and constantly changing through an art that mirrors its cycles and rhythms. Exhibitions with themes and titles like "Elements of Art: Earth, Air and Fire" (Museum of Fine Arts, Boston, 1971), reflected this new interpretation of nature.

For environmental artists, nature embodied and inspired the freedom to forge new directions in art and move away from the commercial gallery system. The traditional art gallery, by exhibiting art objects and reducing them to a commodity, was perceived as limiting the artist's creative possibilities. Environmental artists joined a growing number of artists who created works that could not be purchased. This, of course, opened up the question of support and patronage. Some galleries responded favorably to the new art and exhibited indoor projects by environmental artists. University galleries and museums also provided opportunities to survey these new developments. The most important consequence of artists freeing themselves from dependency on the gallery was their beginning to work in the public domain, a fertile forum for the creation of ecological art.

During the formative years of environmental art, critics and curators often lumped dissimilar artists together, which resulted in a confusion of different sensibilities and tendencies that continues to this day. Twenty years later, it is constructive to compare two works that, superficially, may appear similar, but whose

37 • Hans Haacke, *Grass Grows*, 1969

conceptual basis are markedly different: Helen Mayer Harrison's and Newton Harrison's project, *Making Earth* (1970, reenacted for *Spoils Pile*, 1977, Artpark, Lewiston, New York) is markedly different from Walter De Maria's *New York Earth Room* (1977, based on the *Munich Earth Room* of 1968). Both might have been labeled "earth art," but the material is really all they have in common. The Harrisons ritualize the process of making earth from its elemental components and claim responsibility for creating a life-sustaining mixture, while De Maria uses the earth to alter perceptions of space. *The New York and Munich Earth Rooms* subvert the viewers' expectations of enclosure and ground plane and the customary relationships between interior and exterior. By filling an exhibition space with earth, De Maria rejects the premise of a commercial gallery and comments on the power and politics of the art world. The Harrisons, by contrast, revere and use earth as a statement about human indifference to and destruction of top soil. Plants, the primary component of the food chain, require earth for enrichment. All matter eventually decomposes into the earth, and the process of regeneration is repeated. As Newton Harrison remarked, "effective ritual stems from homage to our life-support systems." *Making Earth* echoes the same spiritual link with nature expressed by artists in ancient societies.

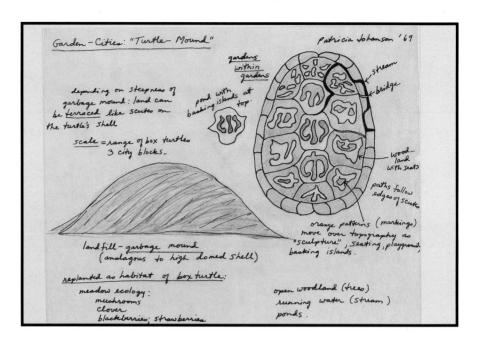

It would seem that the time has come

for the creation of a vast new *public*

landscape. . . . By interweaving man's

construct with the profuse

phenomena of nature — water,

geological formations, plants and

animals in their natural habitats — it

might be possible to shift away from a

world oriented to power and profit, to

a world oriented to *life*.

—*Patricia Johanson*

(from "Garden-Cities," unpublished

manuscript for House and Garden,

1969)

The years 1968 and 1969 were a critical time, during which many ideas and forms were established that would later become realized in more fully defined ecological artworks. During this period, Alan Sonfist was developing his concept of a *Time Landscape,* which reintroduces forests and other natural ecosystems into the city. One of the artist's goals was to elevate disappearing native landscapes to the status of historical monuments and, by extension, to sensitize people so that they could view nature as an important part of their cultural heritage. The work was eventually realized in Greenwich Village, New York, ten years later (FIG. 70).

Growth on a molecular scale was visualized by Newton Harrison, who grew a lily cell in Scoog's medium in 1968. As in many environmental works, the title, *The Slow Birth and Death of a Lily Cell,* describes both subject and process. For two weeks, visitors to the Howard Wise Gallery in New York could see a tangled mass of roots in various stages of development and decay. Three years later, the artist collaborated with his wife, Helen Mayer, in expanding the idea of art as life by constructing a small ecosystem of algae and brine shrimp (*Notation on the Eco-System of the Western Salt Works with the Inclusion of Brine Shrimp*). It was exhibited in the Los Angeles County Museum of Art's "Art and Technology" exhibition in 1971 and foreshadowed one of the Harrisons' most important works, *The Lagoon Cycle* (1972–82) (FIGS. 58–61).

The phenomenon of organic growth was also interpreted in 1969 by Hans Haacke in the exhibition "Earth Art" at the Andrew Dickson White Museum at Cornell University, Ithaca, New York (FIG. 37). In the gallery, the artist seeded a small mound of earth and grew winter rye grass. His simple title, *Grass Grows,* describes his subject and intent. This installation was a modification of an earlier work, exhibited in 1966 at the Howard Wise Gallery, in which the artist grew grass on a 3-foot-square Plexiglas cube. Haacke further developed the idea of growth in several outdoor public projects, such as *Vorschlag Niemandsland (Proposal "No-Man's Land")* (1973–74) for Bonn, Germany, in which the artist proposed that a hill of earth remain undeveloped in order to gather air-borne seeds. Conceived as a homage to natural processes, it intentionally contrasted with the rigidity of political systems symbolized by the government ministry-building complex of which it would have been part.[1]

At about the same time, Patricia Johanson conceptualized a variety of ecological artworks in a series of visionary drawings that offered solutions to urban problems and also functioned as a habitat for plants and wildlife (FIG. 38). In one drawing, the artist designed a garbage landfill as a park that was shaped like a turtle, with plants and intimate spaces for animals and people. It is the first proposal by a contemporary artist to reclaim a landfill, a territory that has recently provided artists with fertile ground to execute their ideas. Johanson's drawings were commissioned in 1969 by the magazine *House and Garden*, and although none of the plans were realized at the time, the drawings became the foundation for her future work (FIGS. 53–57).

39 • Hans Haacke, *Rhinewater Purification Plant*, 1972

Artists also called attention to specific environmental problems through installations in the gallery. In 1969, Mierle Laderman Ukeles formulated her *Manifesto! Maintenance Art* (which was excerpted in *Artforum* in 1971), whose central idea was "the perpetuation and maintenance of the species." It contained proposals for several art exhibitions, one of which, called "Earth Maintenance," involved the delivery to a museum of containers of polluted New York City air, Hudson River water, depleted land, and household garbage. In the gallery, they would be "serviced" — "purified, depolluted, rehabilitated, recycled and conserved" — by the artist or experts in the field. Ukeles's concepts later reached their most profound expression in *Flow City*, which is currently under construction (FIGS. 66–68)

Haacke realized a similar project in *Rhinewater Purification Plant* (1972), which called attention to water pollution in Krefeld, Germany (FIG. 39).[1] This installation was created specifically for the Museum Haus Lange in Krefeld, where the public could graphically see the deteriorating quality of their river, a repository of raw industrial and household sewage. Haacke obtained samples of water released from the Krefeld sewage plant and displayed them in large glass bottles. The installation resembled a laboratory experiment as contaminated water was pumped into a container where it was filtered and purified before entering a large rectangular basin housing goldfish. Any surplus water was discharged by a hose into a garden behind the museum. The presence of a large fish bowl and the picture-window view into the wooded landscape served as a point of contrast between a life-supporting ecosystem and one on the verge of collapse. The work itself was

. . . the evolutionary process for an

ethic is simply this: quit thinking

about decent land-use as solely an

economic problem. Examine each

question in terms of what is ethically

and aesthetically right, as well as what

is economically expedient. A thing is

right when it tends to preserve the

integrity, stability, and beauty of the

biotic community. It is wrong when it

tends otherwise.

—*Aldo Leopold*

(from "The Land Ethic,"

in A Sand County Almanac, *1949)*

conceived by Haacke as a closed ecological system — water was recirculated and not a drop was wasted.

Rhinewater Purification Plant is a political and ecological statement that evolved from earlier work interpreting the phenomenon of water. Haacke was one of the first artists to focus on nature's processes and systems. As early as 1962, he created the first of a series called *Condensation Boxes* in which liquid was encapsulated in Plexiglas. The viewer could see the changing state of water — the formation of droplets and their reaction to air currents, temperature, and movement. Haacke's *Condensation Boxes* established a new direction in art, inspiring artists to bring rocks, plants, and water into museums and galleries.

Although ecologically sensitive environmental artworks would have the most profound impact on the future of art and nature, it was earthworks, another trend within environmental art, that had the most exposure during the late 1960s and early 1970s. The art media devoted much more space to such sculptures as Smithson's *Spiral Jetty* (FIG. 34) than to any other environmental projects. The grandiosity of its scale — 1500 feet long by 15 feet wide — and conception simply commanded more attention.

The *Spiral Jetty* was constructed in the waters of the Great Salt Lake, Utah, out of 6,650 tons of rock transported from an adjacent site. The blue-red lake, stained by brine shrimp, meanders between these rocks and follows its curving shape. Using the spiral, one of nature's most fundamental forms, Smithson contrasts different states of matter — solid and liquid — through art. The crystallization of salt on the layers of rock also becomes an intentional part of the work, indicating the dimension of time. Time is also a factor in the scientific concept of entropy, which fascinated Smithson. Referring to the slow and steady disintegration of systems, entropy is symbolically represented by "the counterclockwise whirl" of the jetty.[2] Ironically, the water level of the Great Salt Lake has risen and submerged the piece. Before his death in an airplane crash in 1973, Smithson indicated his desire to rebuild the work and make it taller. Thus, despite the artist's interest in change and disintegration, he did not fully accept nature's interaction with his *Spiral Jetty*.

Other artists created work that emphasized both nature and art's ephemerality (FIG. 35). Christo's *Running Fence, Sonoma and Marin Counties, California* (1972–76) delineates the landscape using materials that enhance the perception of its forms, color, and texture, which change in response to atmospheric conditions. In comparison to the *Spiral Jetty*, Christo's work is temporary and more public, yet similarly monumental in conception. For a period of two weeks, an 18-foot-high nylon fabric snaked across 24.5 miles of farmland in Sonoma and Marin counties in California. Like the Great Wall of China, it defined sublime panoramic distances and celebrated the technological ingenuity of human beings. From dawn to dusk, the sun's rays transformed the sculpture with each passing hour. *Running Fence* was as much spectacle and performance as it was sculpture. Crews of paid workers spent months erecting the steel parts and three days installing the fabric, inspired by the spirit of community and the drama of the event. Christo is equally interested in the complex negotiation process involved in implementing his work and in its relationship to nature. Each work requires years of preparation dominated by meetings with officials, the filing of environmental-impact statements, and the sale of preparatory drawings to finance the work. *Running Fence* is known to large audiences

40 • Robert Smithson, *Bingham Copper Mining Pit — Utah Reclamation Project*, 1973

through media publicity that becomes yet another aspect of the sculpture. Most importantly, Christo and his team erected the work without damaging the land and offered the viewer a chance to experience the grandeur of nature and of art.[3]

Not all environmental art is environmentally sound nor does it carry an ecological message. The classic earthworks — Michael Heizer's *Double Negative* (1969–70, Nevada) and *Complex One City* (1972–76), and Robert Smithson's *Spiral Jetty* — required extreme manipulations of nature by bulldozing and sometimes dynamiting the earth. These works have been criticized for their negative impact on the land. To many observers, their aesthetic was inherently insensitive, based on the mastery of nature. This domineering attitude was, in essence, a celebration of the status quo: technology subverting nature.

In response to criticism of Smithson's environmental insensitivity, it has often been noted that he intentionally executed his work in disturbed and damaged sites. *Spiral Jetty*, for example, was created on land adjacent to abandoned oil rigs that had polluted the surrounding waters. It was the controversy surrounding one sculpture, *Island of the Broken Glass*, that forced Smithson to rethink the premises of his

Yet I cannot but express my sorrow

that the beauty of such landscapes is

passing away — the ravages of the axe

are daily increasing — the most noble

scenes are made destitute, and

oftentimes with a wantonness and

barbarism scarcely credible in a

civilized nation. The wayside is

becoming shadeless, and another

generation will behold spots, now rife

with beauty, desecrated by what is

called improvement. . . .

—*Thomas Cole*

(from "Essay on American Scenery,"

1835)

art. In 1969, the artist selected a remote, undisturbed, barren rock off Vancouver Island to shatter 100 tons of green-tinted industrial glass. Through art, Smithson wanted to visualize the natural process of erosion that would, in hundreds of years, convert the glass into sand. Environmentalists, fearing the work's effects on wildlife — migratory birds who might perch on the rock — intervened before the project was implemented.

Perhaps as a way of addressing the problems and criticisms of his art, and as a result of his own growing awareness of environmental concerns, Smithson formally expressed the idea of art as land reclamation in his writings. In 1972, he targeted land devastated by strip mining and offered his services to such mining companies as Hanna Coal Company, Kennecott Copper Corporation, U.S. Steel, and Union Carbide, among others. The proposed projects exist only on paper, since industry failed to show interest. Robert Hobbs, the author of a book on Smithson's sculptures, speculates on why corporations may have ignored the artist's proposals. Mining companies were pressured by the public and government to restore land and make it useful for pasture and recreation. The executives at mining companies believed that Smithson's projects did not serve these goals.[4]

Smithson was not interested in creating artworks that rejuvenated the landscape because he felt — as his wife, the artist Nancy Holt, pointed out — that such works cosmetically camouflage the abuse. In accepting the reality of the site, Smithson ensured that the damage from industry would remain visible. Although Smithson viewed mining sites as monuments of their age, he was willing to introduce some minimal aesthetic intervention. His designs reform land into shapes that echo abstract patterns in nature. In his drawing for *Bingham Copper Mining Pit — Utah Reclamation Project* (1973), the largest open-pit mine in the world, Smithson incorporates a map of the surface mine to show the vastness of the 3-mile trench (FIG. 40). The earthwork is conceived as four curving lines that appear to spin in space, small gestural elements that make no attempt to ameliorate the devastation. It is instructive to contrast Smithson's drawings, which abstract and symbolize nature's processes, with his writings, which express an interest in using art to address environmental problems:

> Across the country there are many mining areas, disused quarries, and polluted lakes and rivers. One practical solution for the utilization of such devastated places would be land and water recycling in terms of earth art . . . The world needs coal and highways, but we do not need the results of strip-mining or highway trusts. Economics, when abstracted from the world, is blind to natural processes. Art can become a resource, that mediates between the ecologist and the industrialist. Ecology and industry are not one-way streets, rather they should be crossroads. Art can help provide the needed dialectic between them. A lesson can be learned from the Indian cliff dwellings and earthworks mounds. Here we see nature and necessity in consort.[5]

Smithson's approach to strip-mine reclamation may be compared with that of Harriet Feigenbaum who spent five years working on four separate projects in Pennsylvania's Lackawanna Valley.[6] Beginning in 1980, she sought out sites on which to execute land-reclamation art. At Storrs Pit, near Scranton, Pennsylvania, she designed three projects — *Serpentine Vineyard* (1982), *Black Walnut Forest*

41 • Harriet Feigenbaum, *Erosion and Sedimentation Plan for Red Ash and Coal Silt Area — Willow Rings*, planted 1985

(1983), and *8,000 Pines* (1983) — as artworks that would restore the fertility of the soil, prevent erosion, and bring life back to an area where a balanced ecosystem once flourished. By analyzing the condition of the soil and determining the type of trees most likely to flourish, Feigenbaum attempted to renew natural processes. The trees were also conceived as sculptural materials that would, over time, form large-scale compositions in the landscape. The serpentine design of *8,000 Pines*, for instance, suggested the area's meandering hills, as well as the strata of coal below ground.

Feigenbaum's ambitious projects never reached maturity due to both natural and man-made pressures. Since the 20-acre site required thousands of trees, Feigenbaum, for reasons of economy, was forced to plant small, two-year-old seedlings. Unfortunately, a summer drought and an onslaught of dirt-bikers, who trampled the plants, prevented the project from being realized.

The artist's commitment to art and to land reclamation remained, and her later project, *Erosion and Sedimentation Plan for Red Ash and Coal Silt Area — Willow Rings* (planting completed 1985), continues to thrive near Scranton, Pennsylvania, on a 15-acre site scarred by strip-mining activities (FIG. 41). In response to the site's bowl-shaped topography, the artist planted three circles of willow trees around a pond formed from coal-dust runoff. The sixty quick-growing trees that

42 • Herbert Bayer, *Mill Creek Canyon Earthworks*, completed 1982

the artist selected for the planting were 12 feet high, which helped ensure their survival. *Willow Rings* is maintained as part of a wetlands wildlife preserve. It attempts to maintain the critical balance between people and nature.

Many artists viewed strip-mine-reclamation art with skepticism. The use of art for corporate publicity and image promotion has been questioned. Artists also noted that involvement would absolve the company from fulfilling its responsibility to restore the land. The ethical questions of artistic collaboration with industry were first addressed by Robert Morris in a symposium organized to inaugurate the exhibition "Earthworks: Land Reclamation as Sculpture" at the Seattle Art Museum (1979). The show was the result of an ambitious project, initiated by the King County Arts Commission and the Department of Public Works in Washington, in which eight artists — Robert Morris, Herbert Bayer, Iain Baxter, Richard Fleischner, Lawrence Hanson, Mary Miss, Dennis Oppenheim, and Beverly Pepper — were invited to submit proposals for sites slated for reclamation. The types of abused lands included gravel pits, flood-control sites, surface mines, and landfills. The agencies were promoting earthworks as "cost-effective alternatives to more traditional modes of reclamation."[7] Morris, whose proposal was implemented in a 4-acre gravel pit (*Johnson Pit #20*, 1979), acknowledged that artists involved with land reclamation will be making moral decisions:

> The first thing seems rather bizarre to me. That is, that the selling point was, is, that the art was going to cost less than restoring the site to its "natural condition." What are the implications of that kind of thinking . . . that art should be cheaper than nature? Or that siteworks can be supported and seen as relevant by a community only if they fulfill a kind of sanitation service?
>
> The most significant implication of art as land reclamation is that art can and should be used to wipe away technological guilt. Do those sites scarred by mining or poisoned by chemicals now seem less like the entropic liabilities of ravenous and short-sighted industry and more like long-awaited aesthetic possibilities? Will it be a little easier in the future to rip up the landscape for one last shovelful of non-renewable energy source if an artist can be found (cheap, mind you) to transform the devastation into an inspiring and modern work of art? Or anyway, into a fun place to be? Well, at the very least, into a tidy, mugger-free park.[8]

Although earthworks were envisioned as a means to rehabilitate damaged landscapes, they seldom addressed life-support systems or the transformation of these sites into viable spaces for plants and animals. Based on geometric designs, earthworks were generally not truly site-specific, and they ignored the need for problem-solving and for understanding how nature works.

A few earthworks, however, did take into account the environment and human needs. Herbert Bayer, in his *Mill Creek Canyon Earthworks* (1982), which resulted from his participation in the 1979 exhibition and symposium, created a park where earth mounds also function as drainage basins and seating for visitors during the dry season (FIG. 42). Composed of five geometric elements — two mounds, one round and one oblong; a cone surmounted by a bridge over a creek; a ring mound and pond; and a ring mound bisected by the creek — Bayer's design controls storm water runoff into Mill Creek Canyon. Its success as both an artwork and a community gathering place partly derives from its scale, which does not overwhelm the visitor, and its particular response to the terrain. As part of a 100-acre preserve, *Mill Creek Canyon Earthworks*, covering 2.5 square acres, is a peaceful place where the sight and sound of water contributes a soothing effect.

Although earthworks promoted the notion of art as land reclamation, it was left for other artists such as Mel Chin to fulfill its potential. Chin's *Revival Field* (1990–present), based on a collaboration with a scientist from the U.S. Department of Agriculture, uses plants specially adapted to mining sites to detoxify a section of landfill (FIGS. 96–99). *Revival Field* expands the concept of organic growth first addressed by those early environmental artists who pioneered the notion of art as a living and changing entity. Cultivation as subject matter, based on regeneration and cyclical time, implied another type of creative transformation that seemed to fit easily within the parameters of art making.

In 1971, Helen Mayer Harrison and Newton Harrison began their series titled *Survival Piece*, installations that focused on growing plants (*Air, Earth, Water Interface: Annual Hog Pasture Mix; Portable Orchard; Full Farm; Full Farm Condensed*),

The whole secret of the study of

nature lies in learning how to use

one's eyes.

—George Sand

[Amandine Aurore Lucie Dupin]

(*from* Nouvelles Lettres d'un

Voyageur, *1869*)

43 • Helen Mayer
Harrison and
Newton Harrison,
*Survival Piece # 5:
Portable Orchard,*
1972

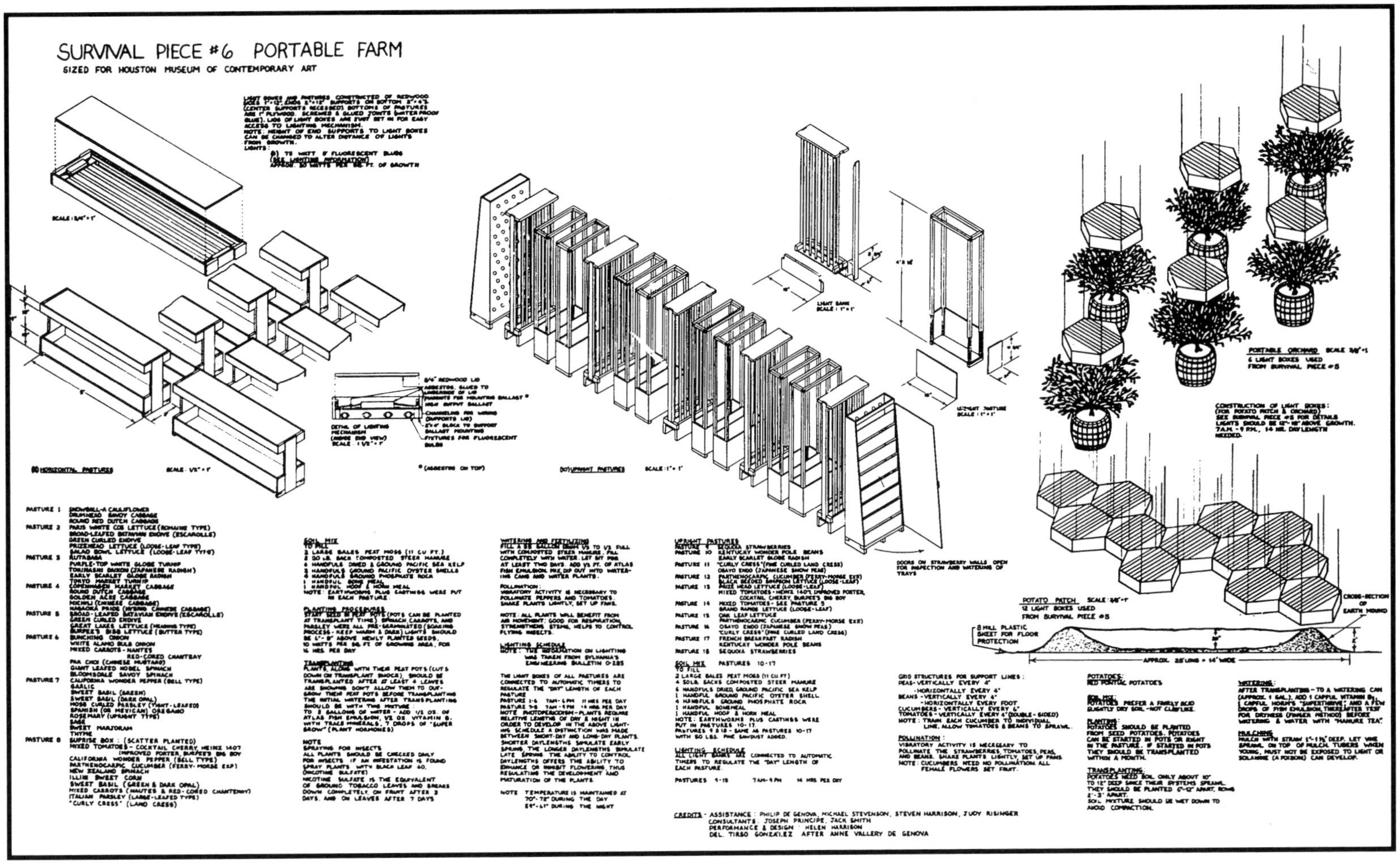
SURVIVAL PIECE #6 PORTABLE FARM
SIZED FOR HOUSTON MUSEUM OF CONTEMPORARY ART

44 • Helen Mayer Harrison and Newton Harrison, *Survival Piece #6: Portable Farm*, 1972

farming brine shrimp (*Notation on the Eco-System of the Western Salt Works with the Inclusion of Brine Shrimp*), and harvesting catfish (*Portable Fish Farm*) (FIGS. 43, 44). The artists transformed the exhibition space into a containerized field of growth or fish pond where the gallery visitor was a spectator to the processes governing life.

These works focused on a once-fundamental human concern and activity. Recognizing that most people in industrial societies are ignorant of how food is produced, the Harrisons sought to create a model of self-sufficiency. Their work attempted to remind people that their survival depends upon plants and upon the death of other animals. Each exhibition was accompanied by a performance that featured the artists harvesting food and sometimes killing fish, which they served to guests at the receptions. In essence, the Harrisons enacted the complete cycle of sustenance. The *Survival Piece* series may also be viewed as a protest against the loss of family farming practices and the establishment of anonymous corporate agribusiness.

Another project that symbolized the regeneration of nature was Joseph Beuys's (1921–1986) *7,000 Oaks* (1982–87) in which the artist, along with his stu-

To forget how to dig the earth and

tend the soil is to forget ourselves.

— *Mohandas K. Gandhi*

Wheatfield was a symbol, a universal

concept. It represented food, energy,

commerce, world trade, economics. It

referred to mismanagement and world

hunger. It was an intrusion into the

Citadel, a confrontation of High

Civilization. Then again, it was also

Shangri-la, a small paradise, one's

childhood, a hot summer afternoon in

the country, peace. Forgotten values,

simple pleasures.

— *Agnes Denes*

(from Wheatfield, Battery Park City: A

Confrontation, The Philosophy, *1982)*

dents from the Free International University, began planting trees in Kassel, Germany for the "Documenta 7" exhibition (FIG. 45). By reforesting the city, Beuys also dramatized the need to revitalize the urban ecology. Any person could participate by donating money to sponsor a tree. As a receipt, they were issued a signed certificate stating "small oak trees grow and life continues." For the artist, the oak personified the fragility of life and the necessity of its nurturance. Beuys's *7,000 Oaks* is only one manifestation of his involvement with environmental issues; he was also influential in the foundation of Germany's Green Party and staged forest actions in Düsseldorf (*Save the Woods*, December 1971) protesting the further loss of trees in Germany.

For Agnes Denes, the tree also becomes a symbol of community, as well as a means to integrate culture and nature. Her proposed *Tree Mountain* (1982) consists of 10,000 silver fir trees to be planted by 10,000 people. The composition, spanning 1.5 miles and reaching 285 feet in height, is governed by a mathematical formula and surprises the viewer by its hidden curves and spirals. Conceived as a "living time capsule," this reforestation project bequeaths a natural legacy to succeeding generations.

45 • Joseph Beuys planting the first tree for *7,000 Oaks*, Documenta #7, 1982, Kassel, Germany

46 • Agnes Denes, *Wheatfield, Battery Park City — A Confrontation, The Act*, 1982, 1.8 acres of wheat planted and harvested, Summer 1982, Battery Park Landfill, Downtown Manhattan

Denes was also interested in art as cultivation and created some of the earliest works on the subject. Her *Rice/Tree/Burial Project* (1968, Sullivan County, New York and reenacted at Artpark, Lewiston, New York, 1977), consisted of planting a rice field, chaining a forest, and burying a time capsule first with haiku poetry, and later with a message to the future to be opened in a thousand years.

A more public and monumental project, *Wheatfield, Battery Park City — A Confrontation* (1982) represents the culmination of the artist's investigation and visualization of the growth cycle (FIG. 46). On landfill near the World Trade Center in New York City, Denes cleared debris and garbage from an unused 4-acre parcel, brought in 225 truckloads of earth, and planted 2 acres of wheat in 1 inch of topsoil. With two assistants and some volunteers, the artist created an irrigation system and maintained the field for four months. During the summer, gleaming green stalks of wheat, which eventually turned glowing amber, were seen swaying against a fortress of skyscrapers. In August, almost a thousand pounds of the grain was harvested. The project was an exuberant and daunting task, celebrating the tenacity of life. By creating an artwork with wheat, a grain planted throughout the world, Denes also called attention to hunger and the mismanagement of resources. Wheat was transformed into a symbol, as the artist's work highlighted incongruities — for example, the crop itself but a few blocks away from the New York Stock Exchange. The activities of the city and the countryside came together for a brief time. After harvesting, the hay was fed to the horses stabled by the New York City Police Department, and some of the grain traveled around the world in the exhi-

47 • Hans Haacke, *Ten Turtles Set Free*, July 20, 1970, in a forest near St. Paul de Vence, France

The Tree of Peace, of course, is the

great spiritual law and it sits on the

back of the turtle . . . We call North

America the Great Turtle Island.

—*Chief Oren Lyons, Onondaga Nation*

(from a PBS interview with Bill Moyers,

July 3, 1991)

bition, "The International Art Show for the End of World Hunger" (organized by the Minnesota Museum of Art, 1987–90). The ecological cycle was thereby completed. This work helped pave the way for one of Denes's current projects, *North Waterfront Park* (1987–present), an oasis for people and nature on a 97-acre landfill in Berkeley, California, which will contain a wildflower meadow, a sunflower field, and a 12-acre wildlife sanctuary.

Just as artists make art of the growing of plants and trees, they also use live animals as subject matter, creating performances and installations based on animal behavior or the relationship of animals to people. Some creatures, like the turtle and coyote, are endangered or mistreated, and artists have thus called attention to their condition and used them as a way to reestablish a bond between people and the animal kingdom. In addition to their ecological message, these performances recall the activities of the artist-shamans of hunting-and-gathering cultures.

In 1970, Hans Haacke purchased turtles from a pet shop and later released them into a forest near St. Paul de Vence, in the south of France, as part of an exhibition of American art at the Fondation Maeght (FIG. 47). *Ten Turtles Set Free* was a metaphorical work, a symbolic gesture, that called into question human interference with the freedom of animals and their imprisoned status as pets. Among the earth's oldest reptiles, the turtle is endangered throughout the world. Ironically, they have long held a sacred place in native North and South American mythol-

ogy. For example, the Iroquois, indigenous to what is now New York State, believed that their continent was formed from the shell of a turtle. Haacke's work was one of the first to dramatize human disregard for animals and their threatened status. By liberating the turtles, the artist engaged in a ritual of respect that acknowledged their value and addressed a fundamental principle of environmental ethics — that all life has a right to exist for its own sake.

The parallels between human and other animal societies was the theme of Alan Sonfist's *Colony of Army Ants* (1972), an installation at Automation House, New York City, which made visible to the public the life of Panamanian jungle army ants. On a plastic and sand floor in the center of the gallery, three to five million ants, in constant movement, used their bodies to build structures rather than tunnel underground. In the gallery the artist placed video monitors that featured people rushing from the subway and ants fording a stream in their native habitat. The work showed that the lives of urban dwellers and ants are both governed by complex social interactions and driven by a relentless sense of urgency. Sonfist provided people with a context in which they could identify with ants, whose tiny size often results in their being overlooked. In addition, the work made clear that their seemingly random movements correspond to activities as purposeful as our own.

Respect for animals, particularly those species that were revered and later abused, was one of the themes of Beuys's *Coyote. I Like America and America Likes Me* (1974) (FIG. 48). For Beuys, the coyote symbolized the American West and the

49 • Bonnie Sherk, *Crossroads Community/The Farm* (Before), 1974–1980

50 • Bonnie Sherk, *Crossroads Community/The Farm* (After), 1974–1980

extermination of the Native American, who viewed the animal as sacred. To commemorate his first visit to the United States, he spent a week living with and establishing a "dialogue" with a coyote. Beuys's performance consisted of "a sequence of movements, a choreography directed towards the Coyote, the timing and the mood regulated by the animal . . ."[9] At one point, the artist wrapped himself in felt and waved a stick in a gesture that evoked "the clear outline of a tall shepherd figure glimpsed across the distances of the steppes." Beuys's posture was archetypal, conjuring a world where animal, human, and spirit were one.

Classified as a small wolf, the coyote is one of the most maligned animals in the United States. Since the nineteenth century, bounties have been offered by states and cattlemen who hope to eliminate them because they sometimes attack valuable livestock. Beuys must have been familiar with the threats to its existence and its unusual intelligence. In his coyote action, the artist attempted to make amends to Native Americans, dispel old prejudices, and close the distance between human and animal.

The psychological bond that once existed between people and animals was also dramatized by Bonnie Sherk. In 1971, she performed *Public Lunch* in a cage with live animals at the San Francisco Zoo, where she ate, climbed a ladder, and took a nap during feeding time in the Lion House.[10] By viewing this work, the audience was forced to examine the confinement of animals and to realize that human beings are also members of the animal kingdom. During the week prior to the actual performance, Sherk introduced objects into her caged space so as not to startle the tiger during the actual performance. While preparing for this performance, she experienced a strong bonding as she sensed the animal sensing her. *Public Lunch* foreshadowed the founding of *Community Crossroads/The Farm* (1974–80), which was one of the first ecological artworks to integrate plants and animals.

The Farm was located on 5.5 acres of land under and adjacent to a freeway in San Francisco (FIGS. 49, 50). Sherk herself directed the farm, which transformed a barren space and revitalized a neighborhood. *The Farm* provided activities and environmental-education programs linking many disciplines. It integrated art, agriculture, local culture, and ecology and became one of San Francisco's first alternative art spaces. Here school children learned how to cultivate and harvest their own food. Indoors, they closely observed animal behavior, becoming familiar with the native intelligence of pigs, rabbits, goats, and cows in a space called TREAT, "The Raw Egg Animal Theatre" (FIG. 51). *The Farm* was a means to "make things whole" by providing a place for humans, plants, and animals to coexist harmoniously.

•

During the wave of environmental activism of the 1960s and 1970s, many artists reestablished a link between people, plants, animals, and the elements of nature. Using a new vocabulary — that of nature itself — artists interpreted the processes, variations, and internal rhythms of the earth. These artworks often changed according to the seasons, times of day, and atmospheric conditions.

Contemporary portrayals of nature as a living force reflect a renewed awareness of its life-generating essence. Artists who addressed the processes of organic growth and other natural phenomena shared many of the same concerns as the earliest artists, who were awed by nature's powers and attempted to capture them through art and ritual. Environmental artworks continue an ancient tradition founded upon the symbiotic relationship between people and nature.

Although all environmental artists contributed to fostering a new awareness of nature, some were more ecologically conscious than others. Within the movement's diversity of approaches and range of attitudes, environmental issues were interpreted and solutions proposed or implemented to restore nature and revitalize the cities. From this new consciousness, ecological art would continue to evolve and expand in new directions.

3

Ecological Art:

A Response to

Environmental Issues

A sustainable society is one that

satisfies its needs without jeopardizing

the prospects of future generations.

— *Lester R. Brown, Christopher*

Flavin, and Sandra Postel

(*from* Worldwatch, *1990*)

THE RAPID DESTRUCTION OF HABITATS WORLDWIDE and the deteriorating condition of urban life have triggered a new wave of environmental awareness. Visual artists, along with writers, musicians, and performing and dramatic artists, are in the vanguard of raising public consciousness about the future of the planet. This development reflects artists' involvement within an even broader scope of social and political activism. Since the 1970s, artists have responded to environmental issues in two ways: by proposing or creating ecological artworks that provide solutions to the problems facing natural and urban ecosystems; or by interpreting or framing the problems through a variety of media — photography, painting, sculpture, multimedia installations, performances. This chapter is devoted to a group of artists who have pioneered the first approach.

Through ecological artworks, artists try to mitigate environmental problems often by revitalizing an ecosystem and the human interaction with nature. They attempt to transform damaged habitats or sterile urban sites into life-generating places. Many of these artists propose or create ecological art for areas where nature's balance has been breached by human interference. Expanding upon early environmental art, these works represent a more socially oriented approach to integrating art and nature. Ecological art does not isolate and interpret aspects of nature but integrates them into a total network of relationships.

By creating ecological artworks, artists are teaching us the lessons of survival as well as celebrating the experience of belonging to a larger community. They continue the long legacy of artists who maintained the vital connection to the source of our creative, spiritual, and physical energies. In essence, these artists are redefining our primal relationship to the earth.

What are ecological artworks and what do they look like? Since the art is in the process of defining itself, there are no clear definitions. It varies in form and result but is often similar in intent. For example, Helen Mayer Harrison and Newton Harrison studied a large ecosystem like the Sava River and its adjacent lands in Yugoslavia, documenting it through maps and photographs. The dramatic visual impact of the work is complemented by poetic description and proposals for solving the river's deteriorating condition (FIGS. 62, 63). The Harrisons' work functions on a conceptual level, stimulating dialogue and remedial action by civic organizations and institutions. Patricia Johanson, by contrast, designs "habitat-gardens" in cities, introducing native plants and animals and sculpture walkways where visitors can experience the natural ecology (FIGS. 53–55). Common to both is a respect for nature's processes and the interrelationships between all forms of life. If an artist manipulates or recommends changes to an ecosystem, it is always to enhance what exists, or as Newton Harrison explains, "to give advantage" to life.

The subject of each work becomes the land or cityscape and its inhabitants — the plants, animals, and human beings who live near or visit a site. Often the artist's presence is not felt, which is intentional, since the direct experience with nature is a primary concern. Sometimes this means that the art is indistinguishable from nature herself, as in Alan Sonfist's *Time Landscape: Greenwich Village, New York* (FIGS. 70A, B). In all ecological artworks, the natural order and the artist's vision coincide.

The twelve artists examined in this chapter and in the accompanying exhibition were selected because they are pioneering a new approach to art and nature based upon environmental ethics. They are among the first artists actively to engage nature with the intent of reestablishing its equilibrium. Works by these artists are as different from each other as are the environments in which they are located. Since each artist reflects nature through a personal sensibility and directly responds to a particular site, each work is unique. As ecological art is site-specific, the type of work exhibited in a gallery or museum takes the form of the proposal or later documentation of a project. The majority of works in this exhibition consist of drawings, models, photographs, and installations.

One of the similarities between ecological artworks is their location in or near large metropolitan areas. This proximity is not accidental, given that urbanization has destroyed native habitats. Many works like Alan Sonfist's *Time Landscape: Greenwich Village, New York*, Patricia Johanson's *Leonhardt Lagoon*, and Buster Simpson's *Host Analog* (FIG. 83) thus revitalize the city by introducing nature into its infrastructure. Ecological artworks that are also urban-renewal projects attempt to heal the physical and psychological rift that has developed between nature and the city.

While restoring nature and the urban environment, artists also redefine their role in society. They become social activists, physically weaving their ideas into the fabric of a community. Often several years pass between the design and the actual implementation of a work. Every stage in the complex process of conception and execution of their vision depends on the support of a diverse group of people. Collaboration with the public and specialists from all fields becomes intrinsic to the creative process. Traditionally, creating art has been an individual pursuit; by contrast, ecological art is sponsored by an institution — museum, college gallery, or state arts organization — and is a cooperative venture between the artist and a community. Thus, the artists must be articulate diplomats for their ideas.

Artists often collaborate with scientists, landscape architects, and urban planners. In his *Revival Field*, Mel Chin studied the technical papers written by scientists on the capacity of certain plants to absorb toxic metals (FIGS. 96–99). He then worked with an agronomist at the U.S. Department of Agriculture to create the first test site for an experiment previously conducted only in the laboratory. In this instance, the artist was the catalyst in the implementation of "green remediation," an important new and natural method of cleaning up toxic waste.

Ecological art provides a unique approach to problem solving and offers artists a new way to synthesize art and nature. Preliminary investigation of the site often determines how the work will evolve. When Heather McGill and John Roloff conceived their master plan for the *Isla de Umunnum* (Island of the Hummingbirds), they first researched the natural and cultural history of the area. Their *Mound* sculpture, planted with native wildflowers to attract hummingbirds and functioning as a fresh-water source for animals, recalls the ancient refuse heaps of Native Americans (FIGS. 93, 94). In this way, the work is layered with information and meaning as the artists seek metaphors and visual equivalents to express the dynamic balance of life. Herein lies the difference between ecological art and land-remediation projects initiated by planners and landscape architects. The artworks transcend their visual dimension and become, according to the artist Mierle Laderman Ukeles, "philosophical spaces." Not only intended as models for ecological rehabilitation, they are also places that catalyze an experience intended to stir the mind and spirit.

Dominating Nature from outside is a

much simpler thing than making her

your own in love's delight, which is a

work of true genius.

—Rabindranath Tagore

(Indian poet, 1861–1941)

That the naturalist's journey has only

begun and for all intents and purposes

will go on forever. That it is possible to

spend a lifetime in a magellanic voyage

around the trunk of a single tree. That

as the exploration is pressed, it will

engage more of the things close to the

human heart and spirit. . . . Humanity

is exalted not because we are so far

above other living creatures, but

because knowing them well elevates

the very concept of life.

—*Edward O. Wilson (from* Biophilia:

The human bond with other species,

1984)

In *Flow City*, located at the New York City Department of Sanitation Marine Transfer Station, Ukeles creates a passageway made of recyclable glass and metal that leads to a glass bridge where people observe the fate of urban garbage (FIGS. 66–68). The artist provides a dramatic context in which to consider materials, their use and potential transformation into another form. The subject transcends its traditional connotations of "garbage" by its connection with the cycle of life, death, and regeneration.

In one project, the creation of habitat and the recycling of waste are integrated into one work. Betty Beaumont's *Ocean Landmark Project* (1980–present), is an underwater sculpture reef fabricated from the waste of consolidated coal ash (FIGS. 86–88). The artist has created a marine-life sanctuary to counter the damaging effects of ocean dumping and overfishing.

The creative potential of the waste problem has been subsequently identified by a number of artists. Many, including Ukeles, are transforming landfills into viable public spaces. Nancy Holt's *Sky Mound* will reclaim a 57-acre landfill in New Jersey into a park, an observatory from which to experience solar events with the naked eye, and a habitat for the flocks of migratory birds that fly over her artwork (FIGS. 77–79). Several important projects not discussed here involve landfill sites like Agnes Denes's *North Waterfront Park* (1988–present, Berkeley, California) and Peter Richards, Michael Oppenheimer, and Hargreaves Associates' now-completed *Byxbee Park* (Palo Alto, California).

The majority of ecological artworks are based on the concept of biodiversity, meaning the preservation of the rich variety of life in any given environment. Since intensive agriculture, urbanization, and industrialization have fragmented or ravaged ecosystems, biodiversity has become ecology's greatest concern. The more complex the ecosystem, the more successfully it can resist stress."[1] Most of the projects address this concern by proposing ways to enhance natural and urban habitats, thereby encouraging growth and the optimal conditions for life. Since habitat destruction is the cause of most extinctions, artists are in the vanguard of this movement to preserve all species, including our own.

Patricia Johanson

*Helen Mayer Harrison and
Newton Harrison*

Mierle Laderman Ukeles

Alan Sonfist

Nancy Holt

Buster Simpson

Betty Beaumont

Heather McGill and John Roloff

Mel Chin

*Cheri Gaulke, Susan Boyle, and
Wilson High School Students*

Patricia Johanson:
Habitat-Gardens

PATRICIA JOHANSON WAS ONE OF THE FIRST ARTISTS to think of art as a means to restore habitats, and her work is an outstanding model for maintaining biodiversity. By creating art that revitalizes natural ecosystems and introduces them to urban dwellers, she has become an innovator in art, ecology, and urban renewal. Although the artist has advanced degrees in both art and architecture, it is the love of nature that has enabled her to intertwine aspects of both fields in such ecological artworks as *Leonhardt Lagoon* (1981–86) and *Endangered Garden* (1988–present). In these projects, the artist focuses on reestablishing and preserving the plants and wildlife of wetlands, ecosystems that are rapidly being lost to urban development.

Although these works were only recently executed, they are realizations of earlier designs and ideas that first evolved in 1969 (FIG. 38). During that year, *House and Garden* commissioned her to submit plans for gardens, one of which was to be built and photographed by the magazine. For this project, she made over 150 drawings that envisioned the transformation of degraded environments into public parks. Although none of these visionary plans were implemented, they were the foundation for the work that followed.

The following year, Johanson designed and built *Cyrus Field* (FIG. 52) adjacent to her home near Buskirk, New York. *Cyrus Field* is a series of paths in three different materials — marble, redwood, and cement block — through a mixed forest of pine, birch, and maple that provide the viewer with the chance to experience nature's changing patterns, textures, colors, and compositions. On a preliminary drawing for *Cyrus Field*, Johanson described her intent:

> What emerges is a series of "Ecology Rooms," where art and nature mirror each other. Themes and patterns unfold gradually, as in a musical composition, and nature is restructured and related to human scale, yet nothing is disturbed or displaced. Plants and animals remain and go on living. The sculpture will grow and change.

Johanson later integrated sculpture walkways into habitats that she had restored, providing a bridge between people and nature as in *Fair Park Lagoon*, now called *Leonhardt Lagoon* (FIGS. 53–55). It was commissioned in 1981 by Harry Parker, then Director of the Dallas Museum of Art, to commemorate the sesquicentennial of the state of Texas. After inviting Johanson to propose a solution to the declining condition of the lagoon, the museum exhibited her drawings and models to initiate a major fund-raising drive. This work sets an important precedent for an art institution playing an activist role in environmental remediation and community education and is a model for other communities to emulate.

The lagoon, over five city blocks long, was constructed in the 1930s as part of a flood-control project. Since that time, the water had become a solid mat of algae, suffocating other forms of life. This condition was stimulated by the seepage of synthetic fertilizers into the waters of the lagoon.[2] Johanson successfully convinced the Parks Department that fertilizing the lawn surrounding the lagoon was detrimental to the life it harbored.

Before preparing her remediation plans, Johanson researched the natural history of the area, which was once a thriving wetland. In collaboration with Walter R. Davis II and Dr. Richard F. Fullington of the Dallas Museum of Natural History, the artist selected and introduced native plants, fish, and reptiles into the

52 • Patricia Johanson, *Cyrus Field* (detail), 1971

lagoon in order to revitalize and balance the food chain. To help purify the lagoon while providing food and shelter to small animals, she selected indigenous emergent vegetation adapted to shallow shoreline waters. Serving multiple functions, the plants' roots also stem shore erosion by reducing the impact of waves.

Johanson also created a series of sculptures cast in Gunite, a type of concrete that was well suited to the design's flowing, organic forms. These sculptures, located at opposite ends of the lagoon, loosely define the roots and leaves of two introduced plants: *Saggitaria platyphylla* (the delta duckpotato) and *Pteris multifida* (the Texas fern). Together they form interconnected paths and bridges that function as observation platforms and seating for the public. One of the large leaves of *Saggitaria* is designed as a breakwater to control erosion of the northern bank, which was losing soil at a rate of 8 inches a year. Johanson has not only provided an effective solution to a degraded environment but, through the use of sculptural forms, has enabled the communty to venture out into the lagoon. Children are often seen

53 • Patricia Johanson, *Leonhardt Lagoon*, Dallas, Texas (originally called *Fair Park Lagoon*), 1981–86, view of *Saggitaria Platyphylla*

romping along the sculptures, observing the plants, ducks, and fish. On sunny days, turtles perch themselves on the sculpture. Functioning as a refuge from city life, *Leonhardt Lagoon* is a "living exhibit" that has been adopted by the Dallas Museum of Natural History.

Another ecological artwork, called *Endangered Garden*, is currently under construction at Candlestick Cove on San Francisco Bay (FIGS. 56, 57). Here Johanson designed sculptural habitats on top of a pump station and holding tank for excess rainwater and sewage that would normally inundate the bay during heavy rains. *Endangered Garden* is conceived as a "baywalk," a nature trail formed to resemble the serpentine silhouette of the San Francisco garter snake, currently listed as an endangered species. The 30-foot-wide path was originally designed to meander for a third of a mile. Along the walkway, made from Gunite, Johanson created a series of gardens where the visitor discovers a variety of images, intimate spaces, and patterns that correspond to different habitats and public uses. Only a few of its unique features are highlighted here, including a "Butterfly Pavilion,"

54 • Patricia Johanson, *Leonhardt Lagoon*, Dallas, Texas, 1981–86,
Saggitaria Platyphylla (detail)

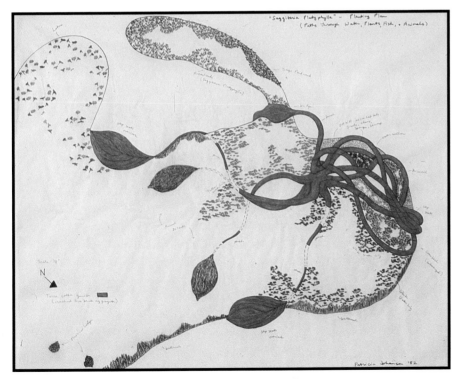

55 • Patricia Johanson, *Fair Park Lagoon: Saggitaria Platyphylla Planting
Plan*, 1982

The lagoon was in the middle of

Dallas' largest park with four major

museums along the shore, and it

seemed a wonderful opportunity to

convert it into a home for native

wildlife — ducks, turtles, fish,

shrimp, insects — by cleaning up the

water and conceiving of landscaping

as food. The 'sculpure' was thought of

as not just aesthetic, but rather a

means of bringing people into contact

with the plants and animals and the

water.

— *Patricia Johanson*

(from Gallerie, *1989)*

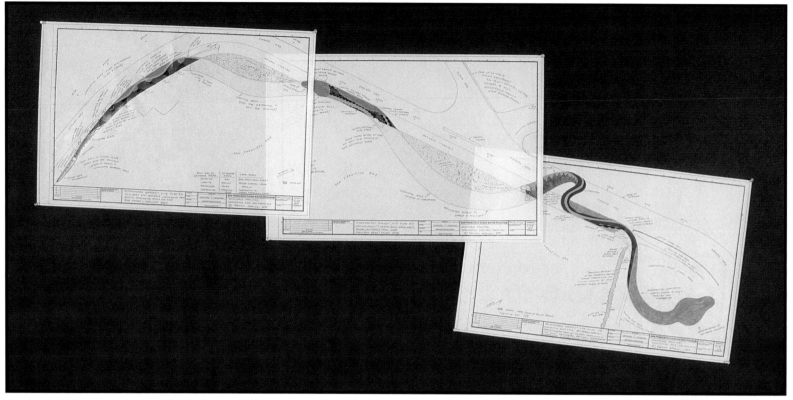

56 • Patricia Johanson, *Endangered Garden*,
site plans, 1988

shaped in the form of the insect's wing. It is located in a shaded arbor that contains seating and frames the life of the bay. The cagelike sculpture of the arbor will be planted with native vines and shrubs as food and nesting spaces for vanishing songbirds. However, the central focus is the bay itself, which is a fragile wetland.

Candlestick Cove is an environment literally on the edge, barricaded by Route 101, the major coastal expressway that divides the marshy mud flats and bay from the San Bruno Mountains. Along the edge of land is Candlestick Stadium and a corporate office building. Johanson's *Endangered Garden* will be an enclave where nature can reestablish itself. The work provides a unique educational opportunity for the public, who will have greater access to the bay, to acquaint themselves with the life and beauty of wetlands.

Johanson's "Ribbon Worm Tidal Steps," shaped like the animal that bears its name, connects the elevated baywalk with the shore. Depending on the height of the waves, visitors will be able to examine small pools of water that shelter a delicate and complex ecosystem of intertidal life. The sculpture simultaneously makes it possible for this environment to coexist with people who will be visitors to the site. Ultimately, the work fosters an environmental ethic regarding the value of even the smallest living things by making visible the tiniest animals of the bay.

The artist is not only concerned with reconnecting people to nature but also to the prehistory of the site; the Chumash tribe once fished here, and their burial grounds and oyster mounds, ancient refuse heaps, were located nearby. Johanson links her design to Native American culture by creating birdbaths shaped like petroglyphs and carved rainwater channels. Originally, she planned to re-create shellfish habitat by introducing a small area of firmer sand and gravel substrate,

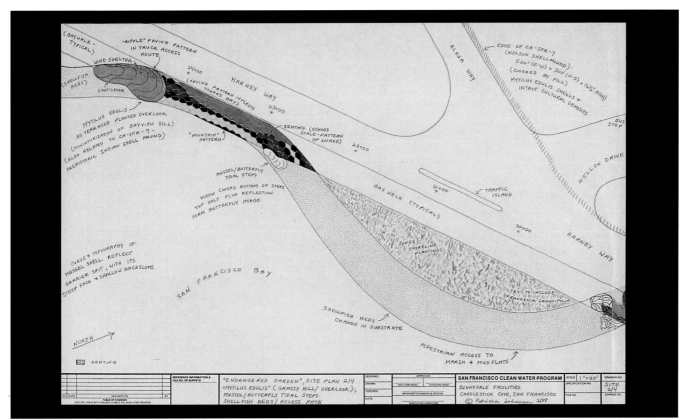

(BAYWALK - TYPICAL)
"RIPPLE" PAVING PATTERN IN TRUCK ACCESS ROUTE
WIND SHELTER
(SHELLFISH BEDS)
CANTILEVER
HARNEY WAY
24+00
(PAVING PATTERN INFLECTS TOWARD BAY)
23+00
MYTILUS EDULIS AS TERRACED PLANTED OVERLOOK (MINIATURIZATION OF BAYVIEW HILL) (ALSO RELATED TO CA-SFR-7. PREHISTORIC INDIAN SHELL MOUND)
"MOUNTAIN" PATTERN
SEATING (ECHOES SCALE-PATTERN OF SNAKE)
22+00
MUSSEL/BUTTERFLY TIDAL STEPS
MHHW COVERS BOTTOM OF STEPS TOP HALF PLUS REFLECTION FORM BUTTERFLY IMAGE
CURVE + TOPOGRAPHY OF MUSSEL SHELL REFLECT BARRIER SPIT, WITH ITS STEEP FACE + SHALLOW BACKSLOPE
SAN FRANCISCO BAY
BAY WALK (TYPICAL)
21+00
TRAFFIC ISLAND
ZONED SHORELINE PLANTINGS
20+00
HARNEY WAY
ALANA WAY
EDGE OF CA-SFR-7 (NELSON SHELLMOUND) - 520' (E-W) X 300' (N-S) X 16½' HIGH) (COVERED BY FILL) MYTILUS EDULIS SHELLS + INTACT CULTURAL DEPOSITS
BUS STOP
MELLON DRIVE
SHELLFISH BEDS CHANGE IN SUBSTRATE
TREES TO INCLUDE FRANKENIA GRANDIFOLIA
NORTH
PEDESTRIAN ACCESS TO MARSH + MUD FLATS
SEATING

"ENDANGERED GARDEN", SITE PLAN 2/4
"MYTILUS EDULIS" (GRASSY HILL/ OVERLOOK);
MUSSEL/BUTTERFLY TIDAL STEPS
SHELL FISH BEDS/ ACCESS PATH

SAN FRANCISCO CLEAN WATER PROGRAM
SUNNYDALE FACILITIES
CANDLESTICK COVE, SAN FRANCISCO
© Patricia Johanson 2/88
SCALE 1"=20'
SITE 2/4

57 • Patricia Johanson, *Endangered Garden,* site plan (detail), 1988

which would have functioned as protective islands for littleneck clams and crabs. These shellfish, in turn, would have attracted and nourished oystercatchers — birds which once lived here. Although the shellfish mounds were not constructed, the main features and concepts of Johanson's plan remains intact.

Johanson's experiences designing and implementing *Leonhardt Lagoon* and *Endangered Garden* have given her a unique perspective on environmental problems and their solutions. Therefore, it was appropriate for Rockland County, New York, to invite the artist to become a member of the Master Plan Committee for the Rockland County Department of Planning. Mandated by the legislature, this committee is responsible for drafting a public-art plan for the area. The site-specific artworks envisioned will address the social, historical, cultural, and natural history of the area. Linked together by a trail system, the works could potentially unify a sometimes fragmented network of ethnic neighborhoods and preserve open spaces. That art is to play an intrinsic role in the future development of a large area of New York State is both innovative and responsible. It is an inspiration for other communities who not only seek solutions to existing problems but to safeguard the land and its unique heritage for the future.

Johanson's work functions significantly on many levels. By reviving habitats and reintroducing native plants and animals to a site, she demonstrates how to creatively preserve biological diversity. At the same time, the artist provides a unique educational opportunity for people to explore nature's intricate relationships and aesthetic patterns. By walking among her sculptures, the viewer experiences the fusion of art and nature and the uniqueness of habitat.

Helen Mayer Harrison and

Newton Harrison:

Poetic Discourse

Along the Rivers

THE ART OF HELEN MAYER HARRISON AND NEWTON HARRISON has expanded over time to encompass large and complex ecosystems. Their work evolved from individual acts that dramatized the elemental components of life and its nurturance: making earth, growing food (*The Survival Piece*, FIGS. 43, 44), and creating a small aquatic ecosystem for raising crabs as an inexpensive means to feed the world's growing populations (*The First Lagoon*, 1972). The artists soon realized that ecological art must examine and respond to the totality of interrelationships that define ecosystems in order to effect environmental change. Their vision thus broadened to embrace river systems and large basins like the Great Lakes and the Central Valley of California.

Since 1977, the Harrisons have investigated various aspects of watersheds and proposed solutions to maintain their delicate balance. Watersheds, fragile drainage basins, are critical in terms of maintaining biodiversity and ensuring the quality of water in light of ever encroaching human settlements. By concentrating on this type of ecosystem, the artists' focus has become increasingly more global, beginning with *Meditations on the Sacramento River, the Delta and the Bays at San Francisco* (1977), *Meditations on the Great Lakes of North America* (1978), *The Sixth Lagoon* (1979), *The Arroyo Seco Release* and *Devil's Gate: A Refuge for Pasadena* (1984–87), *Breathing Space for the Sava River, Yugoslavia* (1988–90), and most recently *Tibet Is the High Ground* (1990–present), which proposes a new form of forestry along the Tibetan watershed, an area feeding seven great rivers flowing to many parts of Asia.

Because their art involves the largest territory of any of the artists discussed in this book, it must by necessity be more conceptual. Most artists study and remediate a particular site, which is often fairly small. By contrast, the Harrisons have accepted the challenge of interpreting bodies of land and water that often cross national boundaries. As a result, their art is as distinct and complex as the ecosystems they seek to preserve.

All of their work is deeply embedded in the story of place, communicated through maps and collaged photographs accompanied by poetic narration or dialogue, and sometimes performances by the artist. As Newton Harrison has remarked, "We are storytellers. Our art is about direct engagement." The Harrisons are concerned with opening lines of communication between the community, civic organizations, and government. The power of their art resides as much in the artists' thoughts and impressions as in the visual documentation of place. With their work, the Harrisons revive and reconnect to an important tradition of communication, which is all but lost in industrial society today. The power of storytelling in societies, past and present, has always been great. The telling and retelling of particular tales have nurtured the spirit and influenced the actions of many great cultures. It is within this context that the Harrisons have created a unique and personal form of ecological art.

An ecological artwork often begins with an invitation, from either an art institution or a community organization, to investigate a regional environmental problem. After firsthand study, research, and interviews with ecologists, biologists, and planners, the artists create a photographic narrative that identifies the problem, questions the system of beliefs that allowed the condition to develop, and proposes initiatives to counter environmental damage. Exhibiting their art in a public forum — a museum, library, city hall — usually stimulates discussion, debate, and

media attention. By communicating to the public the problems that confront a fragile ecosystem and the ways in which the balance can be restored, they exert pressure on the political system and rally public opinion in an attempt to avert ecological disaster.

In *Meditations on the Sacramento River, the Delta and Bays at San Francisco* (1977), the Harrisons argued that the agricultural lands of California's Central Valley will soon become a dust bowl. They contended that the whole system of dams and diversions is ultimately destructive to the ecosystem and to the activities they are developed to promote. The Harrisons directly critiqued government and taxpayer subsidies that perpetuate inefficient, intensive irrigation practices. Irrigated agriculture accounts for an astounding 85 percent of water usage in the vast Central Valley; the crops grown to feed cattle alone — hay, corn, grass — require 50 percent of all available fresh water. The Harrisons used the popular media — radio, posters, and billboards prominently displayed in the city of San Francisco — to

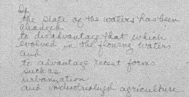
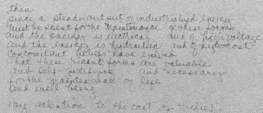

59 • Helen Mayer Harrison and Newton Harrison, *The Lagoon Cycle: Sixth Lagoon*, from *The Book of the Seven Lagoons*, 1972–82

inform the public about the damage to the ecosystem resulting from pesticides and fertilizers, dams and the cultivation of water-intensive crops (rice and cotton) in a desert. Large maps, texts, and performances in several San Francisco museums were also used to promote the idea that human activities must correspond with the physical laws of the universe.

The Harrisons' solutions to environmental problems are sometimes utopian calls to action offering alternative visions of art and life. *Meditations on the Great Lakes of North America* (1978) was a way of shocking people into a radical rethinking about environmental problems. In this work, they proposed an ironic biore-

60 • Helen Mayer Harrison and Newton Harrison, *The Lagoon Cycle: Sixth Lagoon*, from *The Book of the Seven Lagoons*, 1972–82

gionalism that would grant the communities around the lakes more control over their lives. Using maps, texts, and performances, they argued that the citizens of the United States and Canada should secede from their respective countries and reform themselves into an ecological province, not based on traditional political and economic boundaries, and led by a "Dictatorship of the ecology."

In the *The Lagoon Cycle* (1972–82), food production and watersheds are once more intertwined. The artwork, a 350-foot-long mural installation in over fifty parts, also takes the form of a limited-edition portfolio as well as performances. Hand-worked sepia-toned photographs and collage are annotated with the artists'

Sometimes I dream of the water buffalo
in its wallow in Sri Lanka
the one that ran afoul of the gasoline engine
and is being replaced by the tractor
Now that tractor does not replicate itself freely
nor provide milk   nor utilize weeds as fuel
nor produce fertilizer and fuel with its dung

Yet the tractor maker would say that
the tractor is a bold invention
an improvisation that will change the state of farming
It is more efficient
it can cover more ground in a day
It is modern   and cheap
and helps bring people into the technological domain

Yes

yet in some places the buffalo and its wallow still continue
their several-thousand-year-old discourse
their collaboration
and one of the consequences of redirecting their discourse
into the technological monologue   will be a peculiar
subtraction of possibilities   for gone will be the fish
that eats the larvae of the malaria mosquito
while itself serving as a source of protein
and gone will be the vermin-eating snake
that breeds in the wallow's surrounds

while fertilizers will be added
and insecticides   and herbicides

And the refugia disappears
though the tractor is not graceful on the land
and the buffalo will yield to that tractor
although the buffalo
finally
is more efficient
and its dialogue with the land
more lucid

Clearly there is something about
technology that does not like that
which is not itself

Yet this is not
a necessary condition
this unfriendliness
to the land

poetic observations (FIGS. 58–61). Through dialogues between The Lagoonmaker (Newton Harrison) and the Witness (Helen Harrison), an ecological ethos emerges. *The Lagoon Cycle* is a personal and philosophical journey, beginning with observations on the life of a small crustacean and ending with prophesies of global warming.

The story opens with the artists' experiments raising a Sri Lankan crab, Scylla Serrata Forskal, as a model for a simple and inexpensive aquaculture system. Funded by a grant from the Scripps Institute for Oceanography, they researched crab mating and cannibalism in a simulated tropical estuarial ecosystem. But, as the artists point out, the work transcended these parameters to encompass a metaphor for the fragility of all life.

The Sixth Lagoon (1979) focuses on the Colorado River watershed from the Gulf of California to the Continental Divide. Within the poetics of discourse, the Harrisons compare the American system of irrigation agriculture with the 2,500-year-old Sri Lankan system and find that the older system is more effective and less damaging to the environment. The artists warn, "Pay attention to the cost of belief," and the cost of "giving advantage and disadvantage" (FIGS. 59, 60). In the *Seventh Lagoon*, the artists once again refer to Sri Lankan traditional agriculture to juxtapose the processes of the industrial world and those indigenous solutions to environmental problems that have evolved over millennia (FIG. 61). Here, they contrast the role of the water buffalo and the mechanical plow.

62 • Helen Mayer Harrison and Newton Harrison, *Breathing Space for the Sava River, Yugoslavia,* "Then travels through mountains" (detail), 1988–90

We hold that the universe is a

multileveled discourse, a conversation in

many languages — biological, chemical,

physical — most of which we cannot

even perceive, much less understand.

Within this discourse, every place is

bespeaking the story of its own

becoming. Everyone is in this

conversation as is everything.

Consciousness offers us the possibility of

choosing our place and the quality of our

voice in this continuous speaking,

learning, responding.

— Helen Mayer Harrison and

Newton Harrison (from a conversation

with the author, 1992)

Two projects for Pasadena, California, *The Arroyo Seco Release: A Serpentine for Pasadena* and *Devil's Gate: A Refuge for Pasadena* (1984–87) proposed the reclamation of a watershed where all of the rivers have been forced into concrete channels to control flooding. Ultimately, the Harrisons's ideas could be applied to the entire Los Angeles Basin. In these works, the artists called for the "separation of the process of flood control from the destruction of rivers." They conceived a plan to release the water of the Arroyo Seco River from its artificial course and to restore its native woodland ecosystem. In 1985, they exhibited the work, and after public debate and media exposure, the city of Pasadena included the *Devil's Gate* project in their master plan.

In 1988, when the artists were working in Berlin, they learned about the Sava River ecosystem in Yugoslavia, one of Europe's last great flood plains. The Harrisons subsequently explored the region with the botanist Hartmut Ern and Martin Schneider-Jacoby, an ornithologist. The area is still rich with wildlife, including the rare black stork, spoonbill, and sea eagle, and many farmers there continue to practice traditional, sustainable farming. However, the river is burdened by the wastes of industrial production and confined in earthen dams and canals for irrigation and flood control. In their ecological artwork *Breathing Space for the Sava River* (1988–90), they used photographs and poetic texts to illustrate the collision between man and nature along the river (FIGS. 62, 63).

The Harrisons photographed the course of the Sava from its twin sources in mountain and swamp until it empties into the Danube River near Belgrade. The river is still pristine at its beginning and becomes poisoned by the outflow of wastes from a nuclear power plant and factories along its route. The artists documented the toxins excreted into the river by a paper mill and fertilizer plant just before the river enters a nature preserve (FIG. 63). Safeguarding this precious enclave against further deterioration became a priority. The Harrisons proposed making swamps along the drainage ditches emptying into the reserve. By careful selection of plantings, a natural root-zone purification system could effectively eliminate many pollutants. To reduce fertilizer runoff and stem algae bloom, organic farming along the edges of the preserve was suggested. Lastly, water that had cooled the nuclear power plant could be recycled into holding ponds for raising warm-water fish.

Not long after *Breathing Space for the Sava River* was exhibited in Germany and Yugoslavia, the Croatian Department of the Environment approved the plans and the World Bank expressed interest in funding the river cleanup. In this way, their work became a catalyst for public awareness and concerted action.

Over the course of their long careers, the Harrisons have helped to promote and popularize ecological art through their unwavering commitment to its ideals. Their work has succeeded in achieving its goal of stimulating debate wherever it has been exhibited. Increasingly, communities and governments are responding by adopting the Harrisons' ideas into their own long-range plans for addressing the quality of the environment. The Harrisons are also defining the future direction of ecological art by expanding the role of artists who, it is hoped, will become members of teams that implement projects relating to large ecosystems. Their work functions as a cross-disciplinary role model for many younger artists beginning to look at art from an activist point of view.

63 • Helen Mayer Harrison and Newton
Harrison, *Breathing Space for the Sava River,
Yugoslavia,* "To the alluvial flood plain"
(detail), 1988–90

Mierle Laderman Ukeles:
Reclaiming Waste

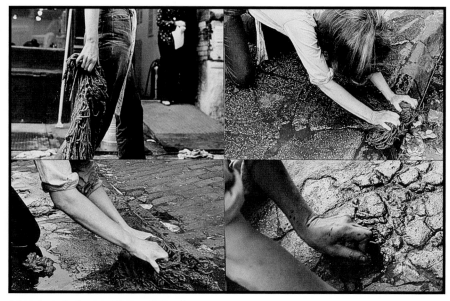

64 • Mierle Laderman Ukeles, *Sidewalk Washing Performance*, June 15, 1974

MIERLE LADERMAN UKELES IS THE FIRST ARTIST to devote herself primarily to the unglamorous but paramount environmental issue of urban garbage. By staking out this new territory, she pioneered an important issue long before it received widespread media attention. Her work demonstrates that waste management — recycling and landfill reclamation — can offer artists inspiration and an opportunity to revitalize the urban ecology.

The advocacy of these ideas and concerns began almost twenty years ago as a "personal journey." After becoming a mother, Ukeles found herself ill-prepared for the repetitive work of child-rearing in comparison to the freedom she had experienced as a young artist. She articulated these feelings in 1969 when she wrote *Manifesto! Maintenance Art*, excerpted in *Artforum* in 1971. Although in this document she acknowledged the drudgery involved in such maintenance activities as cleaning, washing, correcting, mending, she also recognized their necessity for sustaining life. Ukeles's manifesto also functioned as a proposal for a series of exhibitions that dramatized her ideas. In a series of thirteen performances, dating from 1973 through 1976, the artist cleaned a SoHo street and museum floors and performed the duties of all the guards in a museum—and she called it all "art" (FIG. 64). Her radical redefinition of art was conceived in the same spirit in which Marcel Duchamp proclaimed his urinal "art." When Duchamp reused a urinal in 1917 and scribbled the signature "R. Mutt" directly on the porcelain as a gesture of defiance toward traditional art and thinking, he opened up a fertile conceptual field of art making for later generations of artists. Ukeles expands upon Duchamp's example by selecting, performing, and calling the activities of maintenance "art." Liberating herself in this way enabled Ukeles to create a unique body of work.

Ukeles was able to promote her ideas in 1977 when she became affiliated with the New York City Department of Sanitation. As artist-in-residence, she executed some remarkable artworks and dramatic public performances that attempted to heighten public awareness of the problems associated with urban waste. One of

65 • Mierle Laderman Ukeles, *The Social Mirror*, 1983

the highlights was *Touch Sanitation* (1979–80), an eleven-month performance that involved shaking the hands of every sanitation worker in New York City. Working day and night shifts, the artist also videotaped conversations on their collection routes. The event culminated five years later in *Touch Sanitation Show*, two art installations at Ronald Feldman Fine Arts and the old 59th Street Marine Transfer Station. In both, Ukeles combined an array of traditional and kinetic elements — video, sound works, a reconstituted locker room, prints and recyclables — to evoke the atmosphere of the working environment at the Department of Sanitation. According to the gallery press release:

> This immense multi-media installation celebrates daily urban survival by revealing New York sanitation as our primary maintenance system. Ukeles focuses on sanitation workers who she feels are stigmatized because we — the public — are generally unwilling to recognize that the individuals who take the garbage don't make the garbage.

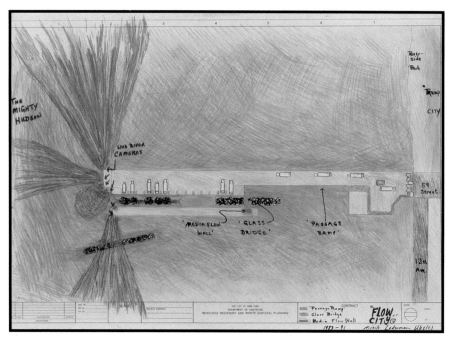

66 • Mierle Laderman Ukeles, *Flow City*, 1983–present

In order to redress this issue, she created *The Social Mirror* (1983), which included a sanitation truck faced in mirrored glass (FIG. 65). As the vehicle moved through the streets of Manhattan, the reflection of city residents were beamed back to them. The people responsible for the garbage glut were cast squarely in the limelight.

Ukeles's concern for educating the public about its role in stemming the tide of waste moved from the realm of performance to a permanent interactive installation in her next major project, which provides an on-site look at the process of disposing of urban waste. *Flow City* (1983–present), located at West 59th Street and the Hudson River, in midtown Manhattan, is more than an educational facility. It is a philosophical place where mundane reality and the potential of transformation meet (FIGS. 66–68). It references garbage, but also a state of being. As the artist explains, "it addresses who we are and where we are going." What separates *Flow City* from a traditional public-works project is the meaning Ukeles imbues in every aspect of her design.

The installation is housed within the New York City Department of Sanitation Marine Transfer Station, where trucks deliver garbage for barging to Fresh Kills Landfill in Staten Island. One enters a shedlike building from the street. As the visitor walks through "Passage Ramp," a 248-foot passageway made from recyclables, the concept of regeneration is interpreted. The materials of glass, metal, and plastic are separated, suspended, and composed in a spiraling format to suggest a state of "potentia," a metaphor for the creative transformation of the material world. Ukeles layers her refuse strata by material, color, and texture and incorporates moving mechanical parts from sanitation trucks. Her dynamic composition is lit by flasher panels recycled from defunct departmental vehicles. Ukeles's space introduces the concept that waste is a false cultural construct; every item is inherently valuable if only our traditional thinking about garbage can be changed. In reality, there is no such thing as "waste." Within the natural world, everything is reused and recycled. Only human beings have neglected this fundamental principle of nature.

Flow City heightens our consciousness about materials; and this is the first stage in effectively reducing urban waste, one of our most critical environmental problems. As the industrial world throws out millions of tons of valuable natural resources, harmful activities like mining minerals and logging forests continue unabated. Ukeles provides us with an alternative to ponder as we pass through a tunnel of recycled wealth.

From the passage tunnel, the visitor approaches "Glass Bridge," which offers rarely seen views of the disposal process — the transfer of garbage from truck to barge (FIG. 67). Ukeles describes this space, integrated into her installation, as "the violent theatre of dumping." The visitor becomes aware of the tremendous energy and synchronization of movement necessary to implement this drama. *Flow City* functions as a proscenium framing the dramatic art of maintenance activity. Her installation is partly conceived as a Museum of Human Labor, a permanent institution that engenders a condition of respect. Maintenance work, according to

67 • Mierle
Laderman Ukeles,
Flow City,
1983–present,
artist on the "Glass
Bridge"

The design of garbage should become

the great public design of our age. I am

talking about the whole picture:

recycling facilities, transfer stations,

trucks, landfills, receptacles, water

treatment plants, rivers. They will be

the giant clocks and thermometers of

our age that tell the time and the health

of the air, the earth and the water. They

will be utterly ambitious — our public

cathedrals. For if we are to survive, they

will be our symbols of survival.

— *Mierle Laderman Ukeles*

(*from* Environmental Action Magazine,

July–August 1991)

Ukeles, is within the cultural sphere and must be visible: "Unless we maintain, we can't continue."

The "Glass Bridge" ends in the "Media Flow Wall," a 24-monitor video bank "floating" in a sculpted wall of glass. "Media Flow Wall" connects the building and its activities — via live transmissions and prerecorded images — to the world beyond (FIG. 68). The primary source of imagery magnifies the connections between the flow of the mighty Hudson River and the flow of waste. Six live cameras focus on the life of the Hudson, an estuary that ebbs and flows under the influence of ocean tides. (The water level rises 6 to 7 feet during high tide.) Views up, down, and beneath the river reconnect visitors with this body of water that has shaped the destiny of New York City. The second major source of imagery derives from the landfill operations and landscape-restoration process at Fresh Kills Landfill, the terminus for all of New York City's solid waste in this cradle-to-grave disposal drama. The third source of imagery concentrates on the subject of recycling, the process that turns each citizen into a sanitation worker. All of these images are composed by Ukeles and programmed for the video wall, sometimes with one image flowing across all twenty-four monitors, at other times with multiple images on individual monitors. The "Media Flow Wall" visualizes the web of life, highlighting its enormous diversity and materiality. The convergence of land and water, humanity and nature is further framed by a view of the river and the Manhattan skyline looming majestically through large windows.

While *Flow City* exposes the neglected but essential work of waste disposal, it also questions our relationship to natural resources and the concept of flux — birth, death, and renewal. Visitors who witness the activities of the Department of Sanitation cannot help but consider their relationship to this seemingly endless stream of materials. By paralleling the processes, energies, and cycles of both the Hudson River and waste management, Ukeles confronts the viewer with two aspects of life — the constructed and the natural. At the point where the two intersect, we are forced to ponder the importance of mediating a balance between them. As Ukeles explains, "We end, but the flow continues. Waste represents the ending of use, it's a metaphor for death, something most of us are afraid to deal with." However, alternatives like recycling and voluntary waste reduction offer an active model and philosophy that emphasize both change and continuity.

In addition to her unique installation at the Marine Transfer Station, Ukeles was among the first artists to envision urban landfills as art. In 1978, she applied for and received two grants from the National Endowment for the Arts to design artworks for several New York City landfills. As in all of her projects, the artist fueled her design with philosophical meaning. One of the proposals, titled *This Land is Your Land/This Land is Our Land*, drew analogies with the way women and land are perceived and treated in the following guises: "Sacred Earth Mother," "Tamed Housewife," "Beckoning Virgin," and "Old Sick Whore." Although these projects were never implemented because the sites were subsequently classified as hazardous, they foreshadow the numerous ecological artworks that are currently transforming sites like them.

In 1990, Ukeles received a commission from the New York City Percent for Art Program to design, interpret, and ameliorate Fresh Kills Landfill in New York City, a 3,000-acre garbage mound that will eventually rise to 500 feet and become the highest land form on the Eastern Seaboard. What makes this art project unique

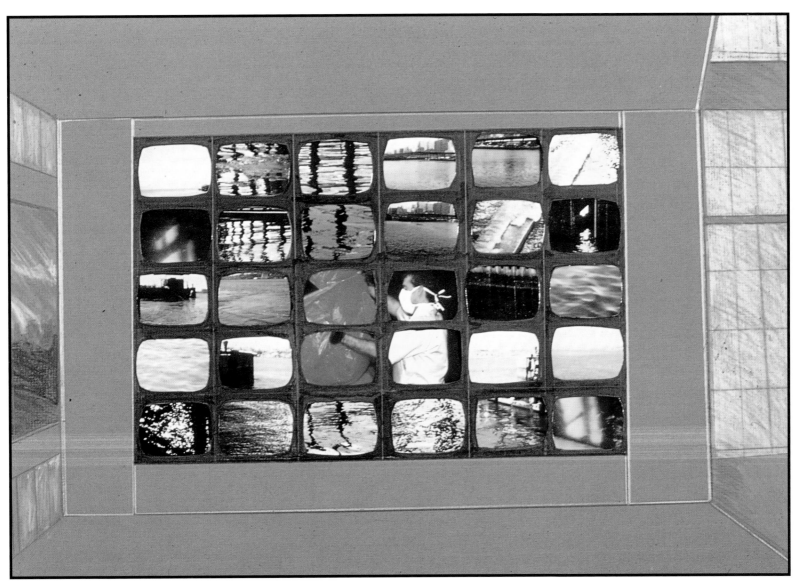

68 • Mierle Laderman Ukeles, *Flow City*, 1983–present, "Media Flow Wall"

is its location, bounded by residential neighborhoods, the largest shopping mall on Staten Island, and a wildlife reserve. After intensive research, Ukeles will attempt to address the interface of humans and nature while charging the site, as she did in *Flow City*, with a new philosophical dimension. For Ukeles, this melding of reality and meaning is what defines art.

Alan Sonfist:
Introducing Urban Forests

THROUGH OUT HIS LONG CAREER, Alan Sonfist has created a diverse body of work in which art and nature often totally merge. Defining all aspects of nature as his subject, he has pioneered many approaches, including: using crystals and microorganisms in art (FIG. 36), interpreting animal behavior, and making ephemeral sculptures from natural materials. However, the artist's most important contribution to ecological art is his introduction of the *Time Landscape*, a monument to nature planted with native trees and vegetation that once thrived where cities now stand.

The sacred tree, first introduced into the iconography of art over five thousand years ago, returns in Alan Sonfist's art as the material for creative expression. Planting forests of trees and shrubs, Sonfist reintroduces nature into urban and suburban communities, revealing the natural history of places that have since been transformed by commercial and residential development.

Although the idea of restoration ecology has only recently gained recognition, Sonfist expressed its physical and spiritual virtues through his art as early as 1965. In that year, he began the first of a series of forest reconstructions in which he transplanted saplings, rescued from a section of a native forest in New York, to a site in Illinois. Ten years later, he began a series titled *Gene Banks* (1975) that foreshadows the current concern with preserving biodiversity. Based on the naturalist's urge to collect, preserve, and document remaining groves of forests, Sonfist assembled photographs of New York City's virgin hemlock forest and exhibited them above a shelf containing jars sealed with specimens. These relics — pieces of bark, seeds, leaves — poetically offer information about an ecosystem that may, someday, be completely lost.

Sonfist's childhood excursions into the few remaining acres of native hemlock forest in New York City have had a lasting influence on his work. Another major influence has been the nineteenth-century landscape painter Asher B. Durand (1796–1886), whose commitment to naturalism was evident in his being one of the first American artists to paint in oil outdoors. Sonfist builds upon Durand's quest for authenticity by using actual trees, leaves, rocks, twigs, soil, and core samples from the earth's crust as the raw materials to unify art and nature (FIG. 69). His *Earth Paintings* (1976–77) involved lifting sections of earth from sites located all over the United States and attaching them to canvas. The color variations of the *Earth Paintings* range from near white to bluish green to deep black. Here, the elements and materials of nature define the content of the work.

In the mid-1960s, Sonfist conceived a plan to return areas of cities across the world to their natural state. Called *Time Landscapes*, these urban parks celebrate the unspoiled landscapes existing before human intervention. The artist believes that nature deserves to be resurrected and commemorated in much the same way as the heroes and events that have shaped both human and natural history. Rather than "taming" nature, a traditional concept in landscape architecture, Sonfist creates monuments to virgin and native landscapes that presently exist as mere patches on a vast, scarred planet.

In 1968, one of Sonfist's proposed *Time Landscapes* was considered by Thomas Hoving, former director of the Metropolitan Museum of Art, for planting within the American Wing at the museum. It was not until 1978, however, after years of research and meetings with city planners and community boards, that the first trees were planted for *Time Landscape: Greenwich Village, New York* located on La Guardia Place between Houston and Bleecker Streets in Manhattan (FIGS. 70A, B).

69 • Alan Sonfist, *Earth Paintings*, 1976–77

Public monuments traditionally have celebrated human history — events and individuals of importance to whole communities and cultures. Now, as we perceive our interdependence with nature, the concept of public art must be expanded to include non-human elements. . . . As the life and death of soldiers are remembered by war monuments, so should the life and death of natural phenomena — rivers, springs, natural outcroppings — be remembered.

—*Alan Sonfist (from artist's notes, 1969)*

70A • Alan Sonfist, View of *Time Landscape: Greenwich Village, New York*, conceived mid-1960s and planted 1978

Since the essence of Sonfist's project is defined by a particular geography and natural history of the region, Sonfist conducted research at the New York Public Library and at the New York Botanical Gardens to determine how the site might have appeared over three hundred years ago. His findings led him to select indigenous species of oak, sassafras, wild roses, red cedars, grey birches, among others. In addition to replacing indigenous plant life, he restored the soil, reestablished original elevations, and included rock samples to the site. According to his plan, pioneering wild grasses planted on the southern end of the site meld into saplings of white oak and hickory in the center and culminate in mature trees to the north. Sonfist's research also uncovered a number of specimens that were not on the New York City Parks Department's list of "approved" trees, those species residents may plant on city sidewalks. After years of successful growth in Greenwich Village, the department eventually revamped their list to include the artist's tree selections.

In *Time Landscape: Greenwich Village, New York*, Sonfist reclaimed an urban wasteland, the site of a tenement building reduced to rubble and engulfed by garbage and weeds. In its place grows a tangle of unspoiled vegetation, a glimpse of

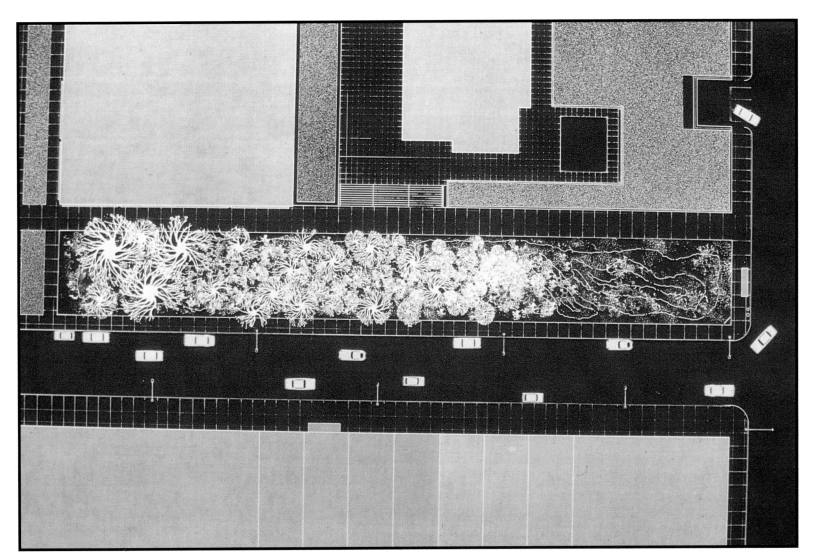

70B • Alan Sonfist, Site plan of *Time Landscape: Greenwich Village, New York*

Manhattan before Europeans arrived on the continent. But Sonfist does not simply attempt to create an idealized ecological model of a forest; instead, he creates a historical, living artwork, a monument to nature's cycles of growth and decay. The work focuses on the process of nature rebuilding itself, which ultimately asserts control over the project's design and appearance. Its very continuity affirms both the values of natural and community life.

Time Landscape: Greenwich Village, New York has become a vital part of the community. Sonfist received cooperation from local residents and schools to help plant and maintain the landscape. For many visitors and residents, *Time Landscape* signals the arrival of each changing season. Even more significant is the artist's message that the survival of civilization depends on its coexistence with natural systems.

Concern for the future — nature rebuilding itself — merges with an interest in revealing nature's past in *Trinity River Time Landscape*, Dallas, Texas (FIG. 71). In 1982, Sonfist was invited by the Dallas Museum of Art to propose a site-specific work for the heavily polluted Trinity River. After researching the geology and biology of Texas, he presented a proposal for a series of natural islands. Each self-sup-

71 • Alan Sonfist, *Trinity River Time Landscape*, Dallas, Texas, 1982

porting island would contain flora and fauna, soil and terrain selected from the many diverse ecologies contained within the state's borders. To accommodate the project, the river eventually would be widened and deepened. The artist planned to introduce a filtration system that would purify sewage and industrial waste. Indigenous animal life would then be reintroduced to the islands and the water would be restocked with native species of fish and freshwater plants. After reviewing the artist's proposal, the city of Dallas incorporated one of Sonfist's ideas into its master plan for urban renewal; it hopes to reconstruct one island, showing the indigenous plant and animal life of Dallas before industrialization.

Sonfist's most recent *Time Landscape* consists of a series of parks in Paris, France, situated along a 10-mile corridor north of the neighborhood of La Defense (FIG. 72). The artist was invited by the French Ministry of Culture to submit ideas to revitalize this area. Three *Time Landscapes* from a series of fifteen that Sonfist proposed are currently under review. As a group, the works suggest the variety of habitats once native to the region. Sonfist's overall design continues the formal axis of space defined by the Arc de Triomphe. The plans for the Parisian *Time Landscapes* are derived from France's most famous buildings: Notre Dame and Chartres cathedrals, the Louvre, and the Chaillot Palace, among others. The artist will reconstruct the topography that existed on each site immediately prior to construction: a pure beech forest for Chartres; a mixed forest for the Chaillot Palace; grasslands for the Louvre; and a marsh for Notre Dame. The land for each park will be sloped and enclosed by walls constructed with stone that echo the masonry of each historic building. Elevated above the surrounding landscapes, they will become Paris's newest monuments. In this city of great landmarks, Sonfist redefines his concept of the *Time Landscape* to include consideration of architectural as well as natural his-

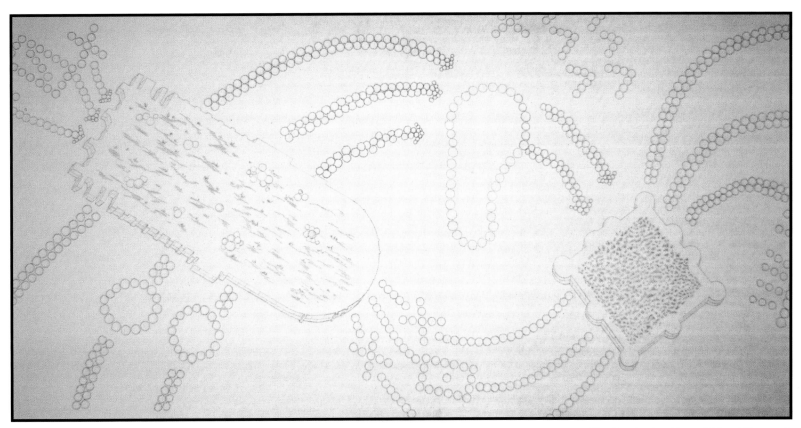

72 • Alan Sonfist, *Natural/Cultural History of Paris: A Narrative Environmental Landscape* (detail), 1991

tory. Once again, his art provides a space in which nature and the manmade monument harmoniously converge.

The concept of Sonfist's *Time Landscapes* is far-reaching; it can be implemented on any scale in any region of the world. In these works, art and nature become indistinguishable from each other and the artist's identity disappears. For this reason, it has become a model, and other artists have reinterpreted and expanded its important premise: reestablishing an equilibrium between the city and nature.

Nancy Holt:
Reconnecting to the Stars

73A • Nancy Holt, *Sun Tunnels*, built 1973–76, Sunset Summer Solstice (detail)

WORSHIP THE SUN IN TIME

WORSHIP THE SUN OUTSIDE TIME

WORSHIP THE SUN WITH NO TIME

WORSHIP THE TIMELESS SUN

—Amiri Baraka/LeRoi Jones (from

Peace in Place, *1979)*

FOR NANCY HOLT, the sun and other stars of the universe are the source of creative energy and become the subjects of many projects, including *Sun Tunnels, Dark Star Park,* and *Sky Mound,* the artist's major ecological artwork. Holt does not interpret the heavens as a static entity as earlier artists have done in painting but instead provides the viewer with a direct experience of its cyclical rhythms and awesome life-generating forces. The majority of people, no longer responsible for growing food and dependent upon fossil fuels, forget that the sun energizes the planet. They have subsequently lost touch with its power to inspire spiritual awareness. Using sculptural elements, Holt frames such phenomena as the summer solstice sunrise and sunset to reawaken our relationship to the source of life.

In *Sun Tunnels* (built between 1973 and 1976), Holt focused the viewer's attention on the sun and stars and the desert landscape near Lucin, Utah. The work is composed of four concrete cylinders aligned with the angles of the sun rising and setting during the summer and winter solstices (FIGS. 73A, B). Each tunnel has holes corresponding to one of four constellations. As the sun's rays penetrate the pattern of holes, the constellations are cast down to earth, appearing on the bottom of the tunnel, as spots of starlight. By poetically heightening the experience of time and the perception of nature, *Sun Tunnels* represents Holt's emerging ecological awareness. Although not Holt's conscious intent, the mystical connection with the earth and ancient peoples is evoked through the image of the tunnel, which was early equated with the Great Goddess and the earth's womb. The transition from darkness to light is a primal experience that conjures the idea of birth. The siting of

73B • Nancy Holt, *Sun Tunnels*, built 1973–76

Sun Tunnels in a remote desert landscape relates to other environmental artworks of the time, which consciously removed themselves from the galleries and the culture of cities. From this very personal sculpture, with its intimate connection to nature and the stars, Holt moved into more socially active projects, which manifested the sublimity of the universe to a larger public.

The sun becomes the focus of a communal experience in *Dark Star Park* (built between 1979–1984) commissioned by Arlington County, Virginia in conjunction with an urban-renewal project (FIGS. 74, 75). Holt salvaged an "urban blight sight," a trash-strewn parking lot covering two-thirds of an acre, and transformed it into a refuge for people, a buffer against the dense commercial development of its surroundings. Nevertheless, the artist recognized the importance of integrating the work with the built environment and selected Gunite concrete for the sculptural elements, retaining walls, tunnels, and ponds that contrast with the natural stones, grasses, and plants.

Dark Star Park is grounded in local history and has subsequently become an integral part of community life. It celebrates an event in the town's history through a solar event. The shadows cast by two of the spheres and their four adjacent poles align with permanent asphalt shadow patterns on the ground at 9:32 A.M., every August 1, to commemorate the day in 1860 when William Ross bought the land

74 • Nancy Holt, *Dark Star Park*, built 1979–84

that later became the section of Arlington known as Rosslyn. In *Dark Star Park*, Holt expresses the connections between cosmic and human time. Since its completion, the town has declared "Dark Star Day," and people from everywhere gather to experience art and nature. Holt's work serves to anchor the community through a ritualized experience of the site.

Dark Star Park represents a breakthrough in public art, since, for the first time, an artist was commissioned as both sculptor and landscape designer. During the five years it took to complete the project, Holt collaborated with urban planners, architects, engineers, and contractors. This experience prepared her for the immense scale and complexity of *Sky Mound* (1988–present), which addresses the problems of both urban waste and renewal (FIGS. 76–79).

In *Sky Mound*, Holt will transform the entire landfill in the Meadowlands of Hackensack, New Jersey, into a public park and naked-eye observatory. At the same time, the artist is creating a habitat for plants and some of the 250 species of migratory birds that visit the area seasonally. At carefully calculated locations on the site, earth mounds and steel poles will be placed to align the viewer's vision with the sun rising and setting on the spring and fall equinoxes and summer and winter solstices. This contemporary Stonehenge will also contain a network of gravel paths, spilling down the sides of the landfill, to further highlight the angles of the sun on these days. In another area of *Sky Mound*, arching methane wellheads will frame the moon in its extreme positions in relation to the earth (occurring every 16.8 years).

Various aspects of the project will be be highly visible as people travel through the Meadowlands on the New Jersey Turnpike or on Amtrak, or fly into Newark airport. Covering 57 acres, the site contains over 10 million tons of garbage reaching a height of 100 feet. The landfill has been sealed using state-of-the-art technology to ensure safety and efficiency. In order to eliminate the possibility of toxic leachate from seeping into groundwater, a 30-foot deep slurry wall has been constructed, a leachate collection system installed, and the top of the landfill has been covered with a specially designed plastic liner made partially from recyclable bottles. A methane gas recovery system, which is integrated into the artwork, has been built as a means to harness the energy of decomposing organic waste as an alternative source of energy for the community.

Sky Mound encompasses all of the phenomenological aspects of the planet: fire (from methane flares), water (from a drainage pond), earth (large mounds on top of the landfill), and wind (causing ventilators to spin). Using these elements, Holt interprets the sublime forces of nature and expands the legacy of heroic transcendental landscapes of the nineteenth century. At the same time, she also synthesizes the landfill vernacular into her design. From the drawings, we can read

75 • Nancy Holt, *Dark Star Park* (detail), built 1979–84

mountains and lakes suffused with the glow of radiant light. Just as the paintings of the last century were intended to instill awe, so, too, does Holt position the late-twentieth-century viewer in a more reverent relationship with the universe.

By measuring time as ancient peoples once did, the work encourages a more profound experience of the cycles of nature. Holt seeks to renew human appreciation for cosmic events by inspiring an instinct that the artist believes is present in each of us — the desire to gaze at the stars. *Sky Mound* will contain two star-viewing mounds. On these mounds, stairways orient the viewer to the rising of Sirius and Vega respectively; and the tunnels, which people can walk through, frame these two stars as they set.

Holt's public artwork is an updated pyramid, echoing those created by the ancient civilizations of Sumer, Egypt, and the Maya. Stepping skyward, these architectural wonders were outdoor stages for the enactment of rituals cor
bound dwellers with the heavens. The irony of a refuse heap servin
on which to commune with the cosmos is painfully evident. I
attempts to create a work that mediates between the debris of tl
sphere and the order of the universe. And yet she does not camou

90 •

76 • Site of *Sky Mound*

The following individuals collaborated with the artist: Anne Galli, Director of the Hackensack Meadowlands Development Corporation Environment Center; Cassandra Wilday and Katherine Weidel, landscape architects; James Mavor, archeoastronomer; Thomas Marturano, Director of Solid Waste.

mound is and purposely melds the vocabulary of art and the vernacular of landfill construction. In this way, the viewer can ponder what modern civilization has created and the legacy it bequeaths to the future. By the end of the century, most landfills will be closed. In the future, they will be seen as the pathetic monuments of our generation. *Sky Mound* demonstrates that we can reclaim civilization's trash heaps into socially useful spaces.

The ecological significance of *Sky Mound* and many of Holt's early works is rooted in a renewal of the human relationship with the cosmos. Ultimately, every ecosystem depends upon the sun and its energy for survival. And while early peoples did not understand the scientific principles involved, they were intensely aware of the importance of the stars, which explains the preponderance of sun worship in many cultures and civilizations. We distinguish ourselves from other living things by yearning for a spiritual experience that will lend meaning to the seeming chaos of existence. The desire to unify heaven and earth reflects this urge and is the basis of all myth and ritual.[3] In *Sky Mound*, Holt attempts to renew this relationship while transforming a damaged site into a life-generating place.

77 • Nancy Holt, *Sky Mound Rendering: Sun-viewing area with pond and star-viewing mounds*, 1985

78 • Nancy Holt,
*Sky Mound
Rendering: Sunrise
on the equinoxes*,
1985

79 • Nancy Holt,
*Sky Mound
Rendering: Moon-
viewing area*, 1985

Buster Simpson:

Urban Environmental Action

80 • Buster Simpson, *Downspout — Plant Life Monitoring System*, 1978

BUSTER SIMPSON HAS BEEN CREATING a unique and varied body of ecological art since the 1970s. He has interpreted such environmental issues as water pollution (*When the Tide Is Out the Table Is Set*, 1978 and 1984) and proposed solutions to counter its damaging effects (*River Rolaids* or *Tums for Nature*, 1983–present). His work also exemplifies diverse approaches. *River Rolaids* is a series of unseen personal actions, while other projects, such as *King Street Gardens* (1990–present), are collaborative and more public. Although Simpson's earliest art focused on water,

81 • Buster
Simpson, *When the
Tide is Out the
Table is Set*, 1984,
detail of fired plate
from an outfall of
the East River,
New York City

most recently he has become involved in establishing habitats that enhance the quality of urban life and provide spaces in which people can coexist with nature. In all of the work, there is a touch of humor and individuality that contributes to the effectiveness of his art.

Simpson's works often ingeniously solve many problems simultaneously. In 1978, the artist conceived *Downspout — Plant Life Monitoring System* at the Pike Place Public Market in downtown Seattle, Washington, where he grew ferns in plumbing pipes attached to the side of a building (FIG. 80). These "vertical landscapes" functioned as a water-retention system for rain runoff from city rooftops. They also improved the water, which had become increasingly acidic from industrial pollutants, before it entered the storm-sewer system. After rain was trapped in the elbows of the pipe, Simpson sweetened it with limestone to neutralize its acidity. While enhancing water quality, *Downspout* provided an ideal habitat for plants and a cost-effective means to solve the problems of storm-water overflow.

82 • Buster Simpson, *Pharmaceutical
Treatment at the Headwaters of the Hudson
River, Adirondack State Park, New York*, 1990,
from *River Rolaids* or *Tums for Nature*,
1983–present

Simpson's concern for water quality, first addressed in *Downspout*, was inter-preted in a work titled *When the Tide Is Out the Table Is Set* (FIG. 81). In order to dramatize the issues of pollution, Simpson visually recorded the effluent pouring from city sewage systems into the rivers. This project began in 1978 while he was working as an artist-in-residence at Artpark in Lewiston, New York, sections of which are situated on a toxic landfill near Love Canal. Simpson made concrete casts of plates used by Artpark picnickers and placed them at sewage outfalls into the Niagara River. The plates were then exhibited with the stains created from con-taminants in the water. In 1984, Simpson continued the project by casting plates in vitreous china as part of the Kohler factory's Art and Industry program — iron-ically, this factory manufactures toilets. After siting these plates at sewage outfalls near major cities — Cleveland, New York, Houston, and Seattle — for a long peri-od of time, they become "glazed" with effluents. Simpson then fired them in a kiln. The plates were often beautifully patterned, indeed the more colorful they were the more toxic were the origins of their staining. The title, *When the Tide Is Out the Table Is Set*, refers to an old Salish Indian saying about pure waters and feasts

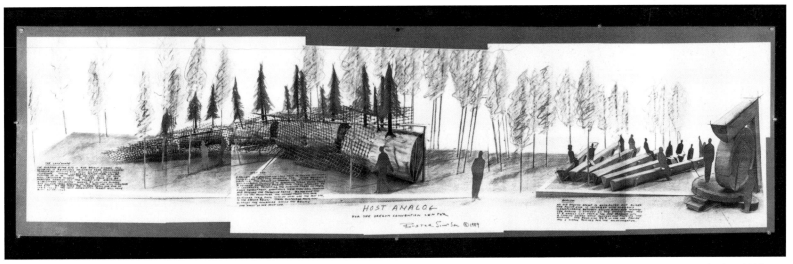

83 • Buster Simpson, *Host Analog*, 1991

of shellfish. It is this poignant reversal of the state of nature — fish from our waters being unfit to eat — that Simpson dramatically recalls in this work.

The damage to water and wildlife resulting from acid rain inspired Simpson's *River Rolaids,* or *Tums for Nature* (FIG. 82). He devised a solution to the poisoning of our waterways by releasing large hand-carved discs of limestone, weighing up to 50 pounds, in rivers across the country. Conceived as "stop-gap solutions," the discs effectively neutralize the acidity of water for a limited time. His first works were launched in the Tolt River near Seattle and in the Esopus River in New York. In 1990, the artist provided this medicinal aid to the headwaters of the Hudson River in New York's Adirondack State Park. In a sense, Simpson's physical involvement in administering these discs, often by wading into the water, recalls the ceremonial practices of Native American medicine men, who heal the sick through dramatic rituals. With *River Rolaids,* Simpson attempts to revive the ailing waters of our country through chemistry and art.

In 1987, Simpson provided an elegantly simple solution to the problems of water pollution, urban waste, and the lack of public restrooms in urban downtowns. Working with county, state, and city health departments, he came up with an idea for a composting toilet, which was relatively inexpensive and ecologically sound. An empty pit would be the site of a commode that, when full, would provide fertilizer for planted trees. Waste would not enter the waters but remain in the ground, where it would nourish other forms of life, a perfect example of recycling.

Two of Simpson's most recent ecological artworks are *Host Analog* (1991), a commission for Portland, Oregon's Convention Center (FIG. 83), and *King Street Gardens* (1990–present) in Alexandria, Virginia (FIG. 84). For Portland, Simpson evokes the Pacific Northwest's rich natural heritage, the huge old-growth forests that are currently being destroyed through timber-industry clear-cutting. He is in the process of creating a forest of trees from a giant 80-foot Douglas fir nurse log. (Nurse logs are fallen trees that slowly decompose and simultaneously become a host for newly sprouted seedlings.) The artist has planted seeds of Western red cedar, Douglas fir, and hemlock directly on the log, which was felled thirty years ago and deemed unsuitable for lumber. A specially designed misting irrigation system will provide the optimal conditions for growth. Although the seedlings will

Among the scenes which are deeply

impressed on my mind, none exceed

in sublimity the primeval forests

undefaced by the hand of man; . . .

no one can stand in these solitudes

unmoved, and not feel that there is

more in man than the mere breath of

his body.

—*Charles Darwin*

(from The Voyage of the Beagle, *1845)*

grow one foot in height in approximately five to ten years, only after a period of five hundred years will the forest reach maturity. In *Host Analog*, Simpson introduces nature into the city while reminding us about a unique natural legacy that has been pilfered. The centuries that it will take to establish the forest contrast sharply with the minutes involved in cutting down a tree. However, the image of a decaying log supporting new life sends a hopeful message about the regeneration of nature that ultimately can come from responsible human stewardship.

King Street Gardens is also an ecological artwork that brings nature back into the city. On an urban site, measuring 250 x 200 x 125 feet, Simpson collaborated with Laura Sindell, a sculptor, Mark Spitzer, an architect, and Becca Hanson, a landscape architect in re-creating the native plants and wildlife of a now heavily developed area of the city. The design is composed of three elements: a marsh of cattails functioning as a storm-water basin and habitat for red-wing blackbirds; hanging gardens, made of trellises with climbing vines of honeysuckle, roses, wysteria, jasmine, and clematis; and a topiary sculpture that abstractly recalls the shape of a colonial tricornered hat, a ship's prow, and a plow. Planted with Virginia creeper, the hat/prow/plow symbolizes man's intervention in nature and his devastating changes to the land. The work will also include a performance space and moveable seating. Plants and flowers were selected to provide shade, fragrance, and a changing vista of color through the seasons, as well as food for songbirds. The artwork offers an experience of nature that heightens all of the senses and filters out urban pollution. In this project, Simpson and his colleagues combine their concern for both urban and natural life, creating an ecological artwork that revitalizes both simultaneously.

The importance of Simpson's ecological art reflects the artist's ability to move in many directions and to respond ingeniously to a number of environmental problems. Many of his designs and ideas are elegantly simple, cost effective, and easily implemented on a large scale in cities around the country. Simpson's personal actions and public artworks together reveal a strongly rooted conviction that the individual can effect changes to remedy the deteriorating quality of urban life.

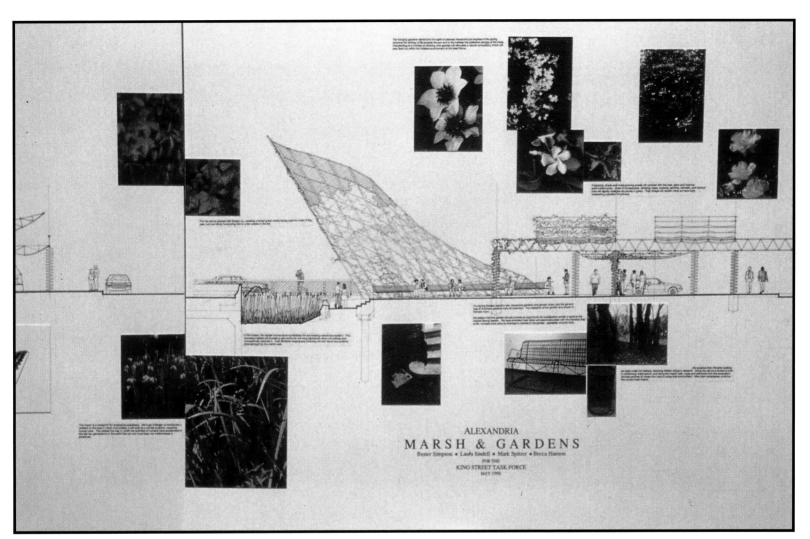

84 • Buster Simpson, with Mark Spitzer,
Laura Sindell, and Becca Hanson, *King Street
Gardens: Section of Sunken Garden, Topiary
and Hanging Garden,* 1991

Betty Beaumont:

The Oceans

For all at last returns to the sea —

to Oceanus, the ocean river, like the

ever-flowing stream of time, the

beginning and the end.

—*Rachel Carson*

(*from* The Sea Around Us, *1951*)

ENGAGED IN A WIDE RANGE OF POLITICAL AND ECOLOGICAL ART, Betty Beaumont has created several works that both interpret and solve the environmental problems facing the oceans. While living in California, the artist found inspiration for her art in the movies, as well as in the land and sea along the Pacific Coast. All of these influences contributed to her desire to work on a grand scale and probe the psychological dimensions of space. Beaumont's fascination with the ocean, its physical beauty and the dream state it induces, dates to her participation as a diver with the Underwater Motion Picture Society, testing equipment for the James Bond movies. Her years of experience observing aquatic ecosystems were reflected first in her photographs of the Santa Barbara oil spill (1969) and later culminated in *Ocean Landmark Project* (1980), which recycles waste and establishes a habitat for fish. A concern for the marine environment continues with her most recent project, *Fish Tales* (1991–present).

In 1969, the country was shocked when an oil tanker capsized off the coast of Santa Barbara, California and created the worst spill in U.S. history. Beaumont, who was studying at the University of California at Santa Barbara, documented the devastation in a series of photographs (FIG. 85) in which she records the technology used to rinse oil from rocks — high-pressure hoses ejecting steam. Although it was soon discovered that this technique caused considerable damage, the hoses were employed twenty years later on the fragile coastline of Prince William Sound, Alaska. Beaumont's photographs transcend their status as documentation of a specific oil spill and serve to remind us of the continued assault on ocean life around the world.

During her early years working as an artist, Beaumont developed an interest in environmental art and anthropology. Her most poetic work of this period is *Cable Piece* (1977), an iron ring formed of 4,000 feet of cable measuring 100 feet in diameter, which Beaumont left to bury itself slowly in the ground on a farm in Macomb, Illinois. The artist monitored the iron's effect on grass growth through aerial infrared photography. For Beaumont, the ring configuration suggested technological and mythological connections with the Fermi Laboratory, a neutron-accelerator plant located nearby, and Native American burial and ceremonial mounds of the Midwest.

In the late 1970s, Beaumont's environmental artwork became more responsive to specific ecological issues of habitat, biodiversity, and the future of industrial waste. She created an underwater sculpture reef for fish in her *Ocean Landmark Project* (completed 1980), an artwork that helps to counter the damaging effects of overfishing the oceans and dumping waste into coastal waters (FIGS. 86, 87). For this piece, she fabricated 17,000 blocks from 500 tons of recycled coal ash to construct an artificial reef. Each solid block measures 8 x 8 x 16 inches. This stabilized fly ash is now part of a thriving 150-foot-long ecosystem colonized by vegetation and fish.

The sculpture of the *Ocean Landmark Project* is located on the continental shelf 50 miles from New York City and 3 miles off the coast of the Fire Island National Seashore. Submerged under 70 feet of water and invisible to the public, the reef and the new life it has attracted have been recorded by the artist in underwater photography and acoustic imaging.

In order to execute this project, Beaumont collaborated with many people — scuba divers, biologists, chemists, oceanographers, engineers — at Columbia Uni-

85 • Betty Beaumont, *Steam Cleaning the Santa Barbara Shore in California*, 1969

versity, the State University of New York at Stony Brook, and Bell Laboratories in New Jersey over a period of two years. She draws an analogy to filmmaking when describing the process: it took months of preproduction work, involving research, proposal writing, fund raising, scouting locations, and meetings with colleagues; but the *Ocean Landmark Project* was installed during the short span of one day.

Inspiration for the project coalesced after Beaumont had studied a test site for a year and a group of marine scientists had researched the potential uses of coal waste from industry, which she later proposed using to build the *Ocean Landmark Project*. Beaumont then investigated a variety of reef-building methods used in Japanese fish harvesting that could be incorporated into her sculpture. When bricks are placed on the ocean floor, their open spaces attract particular species of fish

86 • Betty Beaumont, *Ocean Landmark Installation: The Object* (detail showing model of bricks), 1980

according to the size and shape of the brick. Considerable time and energy went into determining the size and shape of the fly-ash block and how to handle the material.

After Beaumont scouted the site by diving and obtained the necessary permits, she located a factory to cast the neutralized fly ash. Once the blocks were fabricated, the artist leased a barge and tug boat to haul them out to sea. Here on the floor of the Atlantic Ocean, the blocks were control dumped into a configuration forming an elongated mound suggestive of a miniature mountain range whose gaps provided homes for marine life.

The *Ocean Landmark Installation* is a multimedia installation portraying the project through video, a satellite photograph of the site, a collage of soundings images, an underwater photograph, and a replica in scale of the original sculpture

87 • Betty Beaumont, *Ocean Landmark
Project* (detail showing underwater reef and fish), 1980

88 • Betty Beaumont, *Ocean Landmark
Installation* (installed at the Hudson River
Museum, Yonkers, NY), 1990

(FIG. 88). In Beaumont's view, the fact that the *Ocean Landmark Project* is only visible through documentation enhances the meaning of the work: "Fundamental to the original concept of the work was the belief that its integrity resided in its invisibility — it could only be imagined." Conceived to preserve marine life and not as a place for human beings, Beaumont's project is distinct from the work of other artists.

Although it revitalizes the marine environment, *Ocean Landmark Project* is also a conceptual artwork that defines a previously amorphous underwater space and is thus poetically mysterious and, in many ways, unfathomable. The artist, however, does not leave the project entirely to the public imagination; she spent months conceiving and obtaining the documentation. A special hydrophone system to record underwater sound was designed and built to document the launching of the project. Technicians in separate boats obtained echogram images of the installation on the ocean floor and sonic recordings of fish. These sounds measured the growth of the ecosystem and were to be monitored every five years. Simultaneously, photographs and aerial film footage were shot. The artist herself made several diving trips to visit the community of life she had founded.

Beaumont's concern for habitat destruction continued and was later interpreted in *A Night in Alexandria . . . The Rain Forest . . . Whose Histories Are They Anyway?* (1990), an intriguing installation concerned with the destruction of rain forests (FIGS. 89, 90), a subject that has inspired the work of many artists. Unlike those who depict the issue more literally either by exhibiting sculptures composed of scorched trees or by realistically painting the devastation, Beaumont offers a more poetic and conceptual elegy. *A Night in Alexandria* contains library shelves of burned books, themselves made from the wood of trees. A small liquid-crystal display flashes information about the importance of the rain forest as a habitat for a still uninventoried multitude of plants and animals and its potential as a vast resource for people. Beaumont suggests a parallel between the burning and com-

89 • Betty Beaumont, *A Night in Alexandria
. . . The Rain Forest . . . Whose Histories Are
They Anyway?*, 1989

plete destruction of the city of Alexandria's great classical library and the rain forest ecosystem, both sources of encyclopedic knowledge. Her theme updates the one expressed by the nineteenth-century landscape painter Frederic Edwin Church, who experienced the beauty and wealth of the rain forest while it was still unspoiled (FIG. 17).

The often detrimental effect of human actions on other animals and life is more graphically depicted in Beaumont's current work, titled *Fish Tales* (1991), based on updated research she did a decade ago. It consists of a series of flash cards that ominously document species mutated by their exposure to nuclear waste. Beaumont's research for this project, composed of images and text, is derived from the work of scientists at the National Oceanic and Atmospheric Administration

90 • Betty Beaumont, *A Night in Alexandria* (detail), 1989

(NOAA). *Fish Tales* will be created as a multiple to be sold to the general public. It is intended as a warning of the horrific evolutionary life changes that human beings are triggering. Together with her early photographs of the Santa Barbara oil spill and the *Ocean Landmark Project, Fish Tales* demonstrates the artist's intent to focus public attention on, and create solutions to, the problems that face the oceans.

One of Beaumont's great strengths is her ability to freely integrate disciplines and ideas. Her work contradicts the popular perception that environmentalism and technology cannot coexist. In the *Ocean Landmark Project,* Beaumont's innovative use of advanced recycling technology demonstrates how its wise application can actually benefit nature. Central to the artist's vision is the perception that technology can support both creativity and spirituality, and her work is a rare example of this synthesis.

Heather McGill and
John Roloff:
Isla de Umunnum

In *Isla de Umunnum* (1986-89), Heather McGill and John Roloff create sculptures that enhance habitats for hummingbirds (FIGS. 93, 94). This project is their first ecological artwork. The unique context and opportunity provided by the commission have enabled the artists to extend the range of their earlier sculpture by adapting its vocabulary to meet the needs of a nature preserve. Both artists have either used natural materials or the imagery and phenomenology of nature in their past works (FIGS. 91, 92). Moving from earlier installation sculpture to work that is more integrated both in the natural world and as public art was an easy transition for them. *Isla de Umunnum* is an important example for other artists who are interested in expanding their current art to address environmental issues.

The title *Isla de Umunnum* derives from the Ohlone Indian words for "Island of the hummingbirds"; it is located near Moss Landing at Elkhorn Slough National Estuarine Research Reserve, one of California's last remaining wetlands. The state has lost more than 75 percent of its wetlands, an essential breeding ground for fish, waterfowl, and other animals. The survival of Elkhorn Slough and similar habitats as an oasis of life is critical. Environmentalists throughout the world have begun educating the public to value wetlands. Some coastal communities have even taken advantage of their natural filtering properties that reduce the entry of pollutants into the ocean. Once drained, a wetland cannot be re-created. For this reason, the preserve at Elkhorn Slough, with its ecological artworks, assumes an even greater importance.

Sited on a fragile, 5-acre island surrounded by water and tidal marsh, *Isla de Umunnum* is accessible by a half-mile trail from the visitor's center. Like all of the

91 • John Roloff, *Untitled (Earth Orchid)*, 1988

92 • Heather McGill, *Untitled*, 1987

areas described in this chapter, Elkhorn Slough is encroached upon by development — specifically, the Pacific Gas and Electric Company (PG&E) and National Refractories, a factory that extracts magnesium from seawater to construct bricks for high-temperature ovens. Nevertheless, it functions as an important habitat and educational resource with an ambitious public program of lectures, activities, and art exhibitions.

The California Arts Council's Art in Public Building Program funded McGill and Roloff's work, which encompasses a master plan for the site. Central to their proposal is the eventual replacement of the island's eucalyptus trees, an exotic species introduced from Australia in 1856 for timber harvesting, with native Monterey cypress. Very few stands of cypress exist, while the quick-growing eucalyptus has crowded out native species because few natural enemies live in its new environment. Introduced specimens often do not contribute the food and shelter required by other animals, as native trees do, thereby reducing biodiversity. In particular, the camphor-covered eucalyptus leaf "poisons the ground for other plants" and deters insects, without which songbirds do not perch in their boughs.[4] In

93 • Heather McGill and John Roloff, *Isla de Umunnum,* the *Mound,* 1986–90

essence, exotics disrupt the food chain and the intricate interrelationships established among plants and animals.

The artists wanted to use art to encourage the survival of native plants and animals. They collaborated with the Elkhorn Slough Foundation and sanctuary park rangers in order to determine how to best realize this goal. Inspiration came during an early visit to the site, where the artists witnessed the mating of two hummingbirds during an elaborate aerial dance. After researching the natural and archaeological history of the site, they found that the birds, native only to the Americas, were revered by the native peoples, who believed they were part bird and part insect. Fascinated by the scientific and mythological significance of the hummingbird, the artists dedicated their project to its preservation.

Roloff and McGill created two separate sculptures and planted them with native flowers to attract hummingbirds. The *Trellis* is an open steel structure whose center contains the trunk of a fallen eucalyptus tree sheathed in copper. As time passes, honeysuckle vines with bright flowers will hide the framework. Around the trellis are concentric rings planted with additional native food sources, including fuchsia and flowering manzanita. This element in the design was conceived by the artists as a hummingbird feeder, and its wigwam shape reflects the influence of Native American dwellings.

The other sculptural component in the project is the *Mound* (FIGS. 93, 94). Conceived as a half-excavated Native American refuse mound, it includes a semicircular pond that completes the formal composition. The side of the mound facing the pond is sliced open to reveal multiple strata of oyster shells, lava, and coal. From the opposite side, the sculpture disappears into the landscape as a small hill covered with native grasses and California poppies — bright orange flowers that bloom through the spring and summer months.

Reflected in the water, the sculpture assumes new meaning. Its hemispheric shape is transformed into a full circle, an eye into the unknown mysteries of nature. The pond provides the only source of fresh water for the animals on the island, as well as an important compositional element. In order to protect the birds from predators who would drink along the edge, the artists constructed a basket-like form out of copper, which functions as a sheltered island at the center of the pond.

As part of their plan, McGill and Roloff planted additional areas of the island with California poppies. Glimpsed from the visitor's center, this planting will appear to glow. The poppies will attract not only birds but people, both drawn to the shimmering light. The artists also installed a series of paths made from crushed oyster shells, which again refer to the refuse mounds of the area's earliest human residents. These trails circle the island and link the sculptures. In a tribute to the meeting of two cultures, benches are inlaid with the names of native hummingbirds in both Latin and phonetic translations of the Ohlone language.

Building the sculptures and implementing other aspects of the plan proved to be a remarkable enterprise. Since the island was off limits to construction vehicles, materials were transported by wheelbarrow. Throughout the summer of 1988, minimum-security inmates from Soledad Prison and crews from the California Conservation Corps helped construct the project. This was orchestrated by the Park Rangers, who were actively involved during every phase of the project. Representatives from Elkhorn Slough even participated in the selection of the artists and acted as advisers during the design stage. To a large extent, the success of *Isla de Umunnum* derives from the collaboration between the naturalists and the artists.

Isla De Umunnum is the first ecological artwork located in a nature preserve where proximity to human development renders it particularly vulnerable. The work's sensitivity to nature and the beauty of its imagery serve as an important model of art's capacity to revitalize natural and fragile areas. By adapting their earlier experience as sculptors to this project, McGill and Roloff show that creating successful ecological art does not necessarily involve a total career commitment. It requires instead a basic understanding of ecology and of how art can serve the interests of nature.

94 • Heather McGill and John Roloff, *Isla de Umunnum*, the *Mound*, 1986–90

The hummingbird of seven lights,

the hummingbird of seven flowers,

looks for a thimble to live in:

its love life is hapless

without a home to go to,

far from the world and the flowers.

—Pablo Neruda

(*from* Green-Backed Firecrown,

in Art of Birds, *1985)*

Mel Chin:

Revival Field

ALTHOUGH MEL CHIN has only recently focused his attention on environmental issues, his *Revival Field* (1990–present), intended to clean up toxic waste from an urban landfill, has already made a significant contribution to both ecology and the evolution of ecological art. Chin's earlier sculptures were political, referencing issues of freedom of speech, hunger, and misguided government intervention in the lives of people. The leap into environmental action represents a natural progression in which the artist's scope broadened from a concern for humanity to include all living things. In all of his works, he is guided by a quest for authenticity of thought and visual expression.

Chin's first work to address an environmental problem was *The Conditions for Memory*, a series of sculptures that interpreted the extinction of birds native to New York (FIG. 95). These works were commissioned by the New York City Department of Parks and Recreation for an exhibition titled *Noah's Art* (Central Park, 1989). For this project, Chin attempted to capture the emotional and physical loss resulting from the disappearance of animals such as the sea mink (ca. 1890) and the passenger pigeon (1914) by making stone casts of actual taxidermic specimens preserved at Harvard University's Museum of Comparative Geology. By using the mold itself as the sculpture, the void left by the departed species is graphically presented. The artist heightens the dramatic effect by conceiving the sculptures as tombstones inscribed with the date on which the animals were last sighted. The sculptures were exhibited in locations that approximated the birds' original habitat: the passenger pigeon was perched on a beech tree and the sea mink "floated" on a lake in Central Park. With *Conditions for Memory*, Chin ingeniously provided the public with an actual impression of the extinct animal as well as a mournful monument to its demise.

After *Conditions for Memory*, Chin focused his energies on formulating solutions to environmental problems rather than interpreting specific issues for the public. His first ecological artwork, *Revival Field*, is an attempt to demonstrate a safe, natural means to clean up toxic waste from the soil of the Pig's Eye landfill in St. Paul, Minnesota. The project's success depends upon the capacity of a unique group of plants to absorb heavy metals through their vascular system. *Revival Field* will be the first test of this method, called "green remediation," a term used by the scientists who first began experimenting with the process.

Chin became involved in the process of using plants to detoxify waste sites after researching the work of Rufus L. Chaney, Senior Research Scientist at the U.S. Department of Agriculture. For over ten years Dr. Chaney has been collecting seeds and determining their potential in the laboratory; none of his work, however, had been tested in the field. Chin contacted the agronomist and inquired whether he would be interested in testing his work on a large scale. After months of negotiations with public officials, the artist, supported by the Walker Art Center, was granted permission to implement his artwork on a 300-acre landfill that has been designated a state superfund priority.

95 • Mel Chin, *Conditions for Memory: Passenger Pigeon, 1914*, 1989

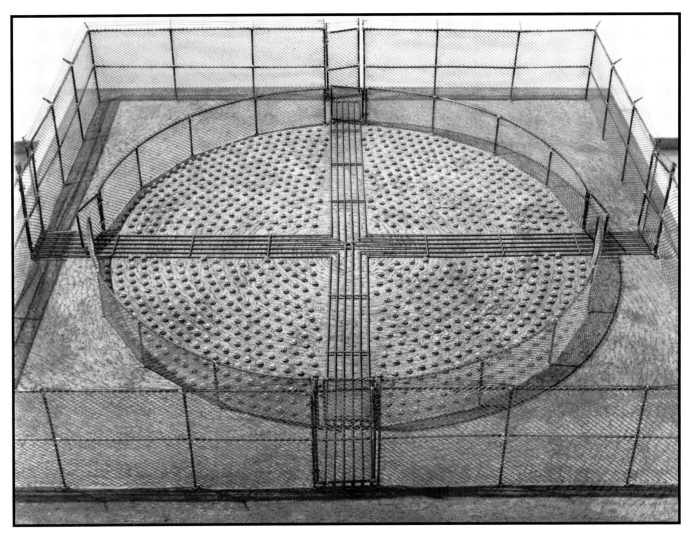

Revival Field consists of a 60-square-foot section of landfill contaminated by such heavy metals as cadmium that have seeped out of used batteries. The planting field is plotted in the shape of a circle, a geometric form traditionally perceived in both science and art as symbolic of nature's purity. Cosmologically, it corresponds to the cycle of time and refers to the four corners of the earth. Whether or not Chin consciously intended these connections, there is a purposeful serenity to the design that provokes comparison with Eastern religious art forms like the Tibetan mandela (FIGS. 96–99).

The contaminated earth is fenced in with chain link and subdivided by intersecting paths that form an X. The project's boundaries are circumscribed by a square. Chin conceives these visual overlays as a target, a metaphorical reference to the work pin-pointed for clean-up. The divisions are also functional, separating different varieties of plants from each other for study. In the circular field, the intersecting paths create four fields where six types of plants and two pH and two fertilizer tests can occur in each quadrant. The land area between the square and circle function as a control plot where plants will be seeded with local grasses. The design

97 • Mel Chin, *Revival Field*, 1990–present, view of the artist plotting the field

98 • Mel Chin, *Revival Field*, 1990–present, view during early July 1991

for *Revival Field* facilitates the chemical analysis of each section.

Chaney and Chin selected six types of plants, known as "hyperaccumulaters," that extract zinc and cadmium through their roots into their leaves and then store these elements in their biomass. Among the varieties tested are a hybrid variety of sweet corn (Zea mays) and bladder campion (Silene cucabalis), which were planted by Chin and a team of five artists and volunteers. They prepared the soil wearing special suits, face masks, and gloves. Prior to their work, they were required to attend forty hours of Hazardous Materials Incident Response Training. *Revival Field* dramatizes the variety of work unrelated to art that is necessary to implement ecological art.

Perennial and annual seeds and seedlings were imported from mine sites in Belgium and England where they adapted over centuries to high levels of toxicity. After planting, the city trucked in water tanks to ensure sufficient nourishment through the summer months. In October 1991, Chin and his assistants harvested the plants, which were cut and dried like hay, ashed under controlled conditions, and then analyzed by Dr. Chaney. Two more plantings are scheduled, but in future sites the process of planting and harvesting will continue until the soil has been detoxified. Ashing increases the concentration of the metal to the level of commercial ore. Ideally, this recycled ore could pay for the cost of the land-remediation process.

Hundreds of such toxic sites exist and could be cleansed by "green remediation." This method is clearly less hazardous than removing toxic soil and disposing it elsewhere. *Revival Field* is thus an important prototype that may be expanded in number and scope.

Plans are currently in progress to create another *Revival Field* in Holland for the World Horticultural Exposition that takes place every ten years. Exposure to an international community will further underline the significance of the work and highlight the fact that Chaney and Chin's project transcends the issue of land reclamation. It tellingly documents the potential of plants to affect our lives in ways still unknown to us. The loss of species everywhere due to habitat devastation emerges once again as an important issue. The preservation of biodiversity is an underlying theme of this work.

An unexpected side issue developed during the process of fund raising for this project. Chin applied to the National Endowment for the Arts and received $10,000 from a special fund, "Artists' Projects: New Forms." However, the former director, John E. Frohnmeyer, rescinded the grant awarded by the artist's panel on the grounds that it was not "art." Although he eventually reversed himself, Frohnmeyer's attitude demonstrates a conservative tide that threatens artist-activism, which has a long history in art. Chin's own description of intent in the written proposal for *Revival Field* remains the most articulate explanation of his "art":

99 • Mel Chin, *Revival Field*, 1990–present, view during first harvest, September 1991

> Conceptually, this work is envisioned as a sculpture involving the reduction process, a traditional method when carving wood or stone. Here the material being approached is unseen and the tools will be biochemistry and agriculture. The work, in its most complete incarnation (after the fences are removed and the toxic-laden weeds harvested) will offer minimal visual and formal effects. For a time, an intended invisible aesthetic will exist that can be measured scientifically by the quality of a revitalized earth. Eventually that aesthetic will be revealed in the return of growth to the soil.

In Chin's view, art and nature become inseparable. This is as it should be since the processes, life forms, and physical configurations of the planet are the ultimate works of art. Accordingly, the most valuable art will assist both nature and people to achieve once again an optimal state of balance.

Working with toxic waste can be a daunting proposition. It involves applications for permits, delicate negotiations with public officials, and most importantly, the danger of exposure. The fact that an artist has been able to surmount all of these obstacles opens up yet another dimension to ecological art.

L.A. River Project

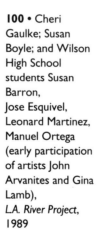

100 • Cheri Gaulke; Susan Boyle; and Wilson High School students Susan Barron, Jose Esquivel, Leonard Martinez, Manuel Ortega (early participation of artists John Arvanites and Gina Lamb), *L.A. River Project*, 1989

THE ARTISTS AND ECOLOGICAL ARTWORKS discussed in this chapter demonstrate that people can effect positive changes in their environment despite the enormity of the problems. Through educational programs at schools and museums, young people also become involved in ecological art and participate in decisions that affect their own lives.

One project that stands as a model is the *L.A. River Project* (1988–89), a multidisciplinary art installation created by students in their senior year in the Humanitas program (sponsored by the Los Angeles Educational Partnership) at Wilson

High School, Los Angeles. Under the direction of Susan Boyle, head of the Humanitas program, and Cheri Gaulke, a video artist, students studied and filmed the life along the Los Angeles River and the dramatic collision between humans and nature (FIG. 100). The video documents the river flowing through an artifical concrete channel constructed in the 1930s to prevent the flooding of new developments nearby. Despite stretches of barren wasteland where the river is reduced to a mere trickle or polluted by garbage and debris, there are oases where plant and animal life tenaciously thrive.

The video installation consists of a twelve-monitor "video river" that poetically reveals a section of the river with a bottle drifting in the rapid flow of water, accompanied by natural sounds. A separate monitor, showing the "River Chronicle," traces the students' explorations along the river's course and features interviews with local politicians and activists who envision and advocate an alternative future for the river.

Included in the original installation were photographs and a map documenting the students' forays along the river; a video compilation of Hollywood movie scenes filmed nearby; a shopping cart filled with plastic, tires, and other garbage dumped into the water and collected by students; and a large painting by Manuel Ortega interpreting the graffiti scrawled along the concrete. Historical photographs of the river taken at the turn of the century were exhibited and a laboratory flask of water from the river was analyzed and displayed to reveal its contaminants.

The *L.A. River Project* is more than an art installation or study of contrasts. It provided students with the opportunity to become involved in regional issues through an interdisciplinary approach that integrated history, literature, politics, natural science, and art. Students learned how to use video as both documentation and art. They were responsible for all of the shooting and editing of the *L.A. River Project*. As part of their research, they examined the history of the river, the initial rationale behind the flood-control plan, and contemporary views regarding water-management policies. Another important part of the process was the students' direct observation of the river and the formulation of their own solutions to the problems facing this urban waterway. They visualized the river's future in an architectural rendering (FIG. 101). Humanitas students in an architectural drafting class collaborated to create this work that shows the river transformed into a park with trees, bike paths, and art.

The success of the *L.A. River Project* derives from its interdisciplinary focus, which was rooted in the reality of an environmental problem that directly affected the students' lives. The program and the art that evolved is a prototype for other educational institutions that seek to stimulate creative and critical thinking.

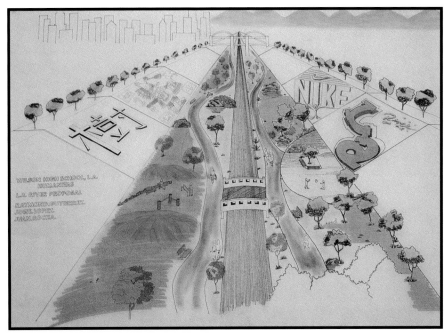

101 • *L.A. River Project: Vision of the Future,* 1989, colored architectural rendering on paper by Ray Gutierrez, Josie Lopez, and Juan Rocha

The ethics of reverence for life makes

no distinction between higher and

lower, more precious and less precious

lives. It has good reasons for this

omission. For what are we doing, when

we establish hard and fast gradations in

value between living organisms, but

judging them in relation to ourselves,

by whether they seem to stand closer

to us or farther from us. This is a

wholly subjective standard. How can

we know what importance other living

organisms have in themselves and in

terms of the universe?

—Albert Schweitzer (from *The*

Teaching of Reverence for Life, 1965)

•

THE DETERIORATING PHYSICAL CONDITION OF THE PLANET and the diminishing quality of life have challenged artists to seek solutions to the current environmental crisis. Ecological art has become a catalyst for a heightened awareness of nature as well as a model of interdisciplinary problem-solving. By revitalizing and recreating habitats, artists redefine their role in society as their art becomes inseparable from life itself. In ancient times, artists mediated between people and the world of plants and animals; today many artists actually remediate the environment and help close the gap between nature and humanity.

By introducing native plants and animals into a site, artists stimulate biodiversity. Forests and marshes, two types of habitats vanishing around the world, are recreated on city streets or are rejuvenated in parks or nature preserves. Most of these works are conceived as sanctuaries where human beings can experience nature's energy and beauty as sources of physical and spiritual renewal.

Artists also transform the problem of waste, one of the most pressing concerns of urban ecology, into a fertile ground for art. Landfills are becoming art parks for people and wildlife, and the creative potential of recycling is harnessed to establish habitats, clean toxic dumps, and alter traditional public perceptions of urban waste.

These diverse artworks help crystallize a new environmental ethic whereby humans live harmoniously within a larger community of life. Consequently, the educational component and advocacy stance of ecological art are as significant as its visual and ecological impact. They serve as examples of how the individual can effect positive environmental change. By reviving urban and natural environments, artists attempt to stimulate a reverence for life with the hope that others will also nurture its vitality.

THE ARTISTS ENGAGED IN ECOLOGICAL ART are our contemporary shamans. Through their work, they attempt to heal the rift that has developed between people and nature. Like many of the early artists before them, they seek to restore balance in a world whose natural vitality is rapidly being sapped.

As the environment was radically altered by human development through the ages, achieving harmony with nature became ever more crucial. The earliest artists appropriated images from nature — animals, the sacred tree, the goddess figure, landscapes — to express its regenerative powers. Along with ritual and myth, their art inspired respect for life. Humanity has recently unleashed an assault against nature on a scale that has never before been matched. Many contemporary artists are responding, like their earlier counterparts, by communicating the restorative powers of nature. However, today's artists do not refer to nature symbolically through painting and sculpture but actually through site-specific works that attempt to re-create natural ecosystems and revive urban ecologies. In the past, landscape painting reconnected urban dwellers with nature; today, artists design more direct and physical contexts for reintroducing the natural world to the city. Ultimately, all of these works are based on an ethos that respects the sanctity of life.

Although rooted in tradition, ecological art is a relatively recent phenomenon. Emerging in the late 1960s, it is slowly beginning to make an impact as it provides solutions to environmental problems. The works enlarge the scope and methods of the creative process by integrating a wide breadth of knowledge into a holistic approach to problem solving. Ecological artworks are models for interdisciplinary environmental action. This new approach to art often requires the complex implementation of large public projects involving community interaction. In contrast to the traditional, relatively solitary creation of paintings or sculpture, ecological art depends upon a wide network of relationships for its execution.

By abandoning the isolation of the studio, ecological artists are expanding the definition of art and forging a new identity for themselves. Although this development might be seen as revolutionary, in fact, like many movements in art history, it expands the definition of art to include new styles and subjects. In order to express the complexities of each age, artists have had to stretch traditional boundaries; artists today have succeeded in formulating unique art forms in their quest to restore ecological balance and enhance the natural environment.

By supporting ecological art, museums also have an opportunity to redefine themselves and reshape the perceptions of their audiences. When museums were made public in the late eighteenth century, they were mainly repositories for objects of contemplation. This has been their emphasis for two centuries. Indeed, in more recent times, museums have weathered criticism for exhibiting art divorced from its context and for functioning at a distance from the public. Sponsoring ecological art gives museums the opportunity to play an activist role in the community. In addition to studying, conserving, and displaying more traditional forms of art, their activities can expand into direct involvement in the restoration of nature.

Art is defined through the process of creation, and ecological art consummately expresses this by enhancing the foundations of life. In reality, nature is our greatest masterpiece — fragile and requiring protection. While working to preserve this threatened treasure, artists demonstrate how people can effect positive environmental change.

Postscript

Notes

Chapter 1

1. Andrew Goudie, "The Changing Human Impact," in *The Fragile Environment*, ed. Laurie Friday and Ronald Laskey, p. 4.

2. Historians speculate that art existed elsewhere — in regions of China and Africa — but has probably perished due to exposure to climate.

3. See Mircea Eliade, ed., *The Encyclopedia of Religion*, vol. 1, p. 294.

4. André Leroi-Gourhan, *Treasures of Prehistoric Art*, pp. 172–74.

5. See Mario Ruspoli, *The Cave of Lascaux*, p. 33. The extinction of bison coincides with the end of the ice age, when milder climate ensued and forests started usurping the grazing lands of horses and bison.

6. See Andrew Goudie, p. 8. Goudie discusses the possibility of overhunting of large mammals by man. The introduction of spears and bows and arrows as well as the fact that large animals reproduce slowly are some of the arguments in favor of what has come to be called "Pleistocene overkill."

7. From the animal bones discovered by archaeologists, it has been determined that people's main source of protein was reindeer, which were not frequently depicted in the caves.

8. According to James George Frazer in *The Golden Bough*, pp. 19–20, tribes in central Australia maintained their food supply through magical ceremonies intended to multiply their totemic animals. Frazier also describes the belief in the transfer of the soul of the human being to the animal.

9. See Allen Wardwell, *Objects of Bright Pride*, pp. 82–83. Raven rattles were used by chiefs for social ceremonies.

10. See John Reader, *Mankind on Earth*, pp. 190–91.

11. According to I. G. Simmons, *Changing the Face of the Earth*, p. 94, the soil in Mesopotamia became so saline from irrigation that land was removed from cultivation, resulting in a plummeting grain harvest.

12. *Ibid.*, p. 177.

13. The Metropolitan Museum of Art, New York, contains a large display of relief sculptures of the sacred tree in southwest Asia.

14. See Mircea Eliade, ed., *The Encyclopedia of Religion*, vol. 15, pp. 26–32, for a short summary of the significance of the sacred tree in religion. An exhibition, organized by Steven C. Rockefeller and John C. Elder, for Middlebury College in Vermont, called *Spirit and Nature* (1990) was organized around the concept of the sacred tree.

15. See Erich Neumann, *The Great Mother*, pp. 241–42 for an extended discussion of this image.

16. Charles Gallenkamp, *Maya*, p. 107.

17. Marija Gimbutas, *The Language of the Goddess*, p. 121, also interprets the snake as "interchangeable with the tree of life."

18. Carolyn Merchant, *The Death of Nature*, p. 4.

19. I. G. Simmons, *Changing the Face of the Earth*, p. 116. Simmons describes the results of deforestation in Rome, which seems very similar to conditions existing today: silting, loss of habitat, floods. He mentions the work of J. D. Hughes and J. V. Thirgood, two environmental historians who have reached this conclusion in an article entitled "Deforestation in Ancient Greece and Rome: A Cause of Collapse?" in the *Ecologist* 12, 1982, pp. 196–208.

20. Albert E. Elsen, *Purposes of Art*, p. 298.

21. A few saints, most notably St. Francis, rejected this attitude and attracted a sizeable following. Giovanni Bellini's *St. Francis in the Desert* (1485, The Frick Collection, New York) portrays the saint in a rocky landscape among the animals he so loved. The enlightenment that comes from a communion with nature is experienced by the viewer, not directly, but through the figure of the saint, which dominates the scene. The city, visible in the distance, is a reminder of civilized culture.

22. Nenner exhibited *Crucified Coyote* in 1981 at the Arsenal Building in Central Park as part of an exhibition, *Animals in the Arsenal*. She was forced by authorities to remove it after several organizations protested against its "gruesome" imagery.

23. See Carolyn Merchant, *The Death of Nature*, pp. 220–27.

24. See Barbara Novak, *Nature and Culture*, pp. 157–165 and Nicolai Cikovsky Jr., "The Ravages of the Axe: The Meaning of the Tree Stump in Nineteenth-Century American Art," *Art Bulletin*, Vol. LXI, No. 4, December 1979, pp. 611ff. for an extended discussion of this subject.

25. A recent exhibition at the National Museum of American Art, "The West as America: Reinterpreting Images of the Frontier, 1820–1920," 1991–92, examined the role of the artist in perpetuating the myth that pioneering could both exploit and maintain the natural world.

26. See Frederick Law Olmsted, Jr. and Theodora Kimball, eds., *Forty Years of Landscape Architecture: Central Park*, pp. 22–23.

27. *Ibid*, pp. 45–46.

28. These distinctions were made by Olmsted himself in his address "The Justifying Value of a Public Park" (1870).

29. An exhibition that examined this trend was organized by the Brooklyn Museum; see: *The American Renaissance 1876–1917*, exh. cat., The Brooklyn Museum, New York, 1979.

30. Donald Worster, a native son, examines the history of the area and the manmade disturbances that caused the Dust Bowl in his book, *Dust Bowl: The Southern Plains in the 1930's*. The following environmental descriptions summarize his account.

31. Rachel Carson, *Silent Spring*, p. 174.

Chapter 2

1. See *Hans Haacke: Unfinished Business*, exh. cat., The New Museum of Contemporary Art, pp. 106–07.

2. See Robert Hobbs, *Robert Smithson: Sculpture*, pp. 191–97 for an analysis of *Spiral Jetty*.

3. Christo completed an environmental-impact statement in order to satisfy public officials about the work's benign effect on the landscape. While his permit to plunge the work into the Pacific Ocean as a grand finale was pending review, the artist proceeded to complete the work. Christo was criticized for circumventing this aspect of the regulation. See John Beardsley, *Earthworks and Beyond*, 1989, p. 34.

4. Robert Hobbs, *Robert Smithson: Sculpture*, pp. 215–27 for discussion of the artist's reclamation projects.

5. Written 1971 and published in: *The Writings of Robert Smithson*, ed. Nancy Holt, p. 220.

6. For an analysis of Feigenbaum's projects, see: Ann Murray, "Pits and Pitfalls: Harriet Feigenbaum's Reclamation Art," *Woman's Art Journal*, Spring/Summer 1991, pp. 29–35.

7. See foreword to *Earthworks: Land Reclamation as Sculpture*, exh. cat., p. 7.

8. *Earthworks: Land Reclamation as Sculpture*, pp. 16–17.

9. The coyote action is described at length by Caroline Tisdall in *Joseph Beuys*, exh. cat., The Solomon R. Guggenheim Museum, New York, 1979, pp. 228–35.

10. See interview with Bonnie Sherk by Linda Frye Burnham in *High Performance*, Fall 1981, pp. 49ff.

Chapter 3

1. Barry Commoner, *The Closing Circle*, pp. 38–39.

2. Eutrophication — the process by which nutrients from fertilizers stimulate the bloom of algae — is becoming rampant worldwide, resulting in the suffocation of life in many coastal waters and great lakes, including Lake Erie.

3. Joseph Campbell, *The Masks of God: Primitive Mythology*, pp. 146–50.

4. Mark Silberstein and Eileen Campbell, *Elkhorn Slough*, p. 22.

Betty Beaumont

Steam Cleaning the Santa Barbara Shore in California, 1969
black-and-white photograph
11 × 14 in.
Courtesy the artist

Ocean Landmark Installation, 1980
combined-media installation documenting the *Ocean Landmark Project*, an underwater sculpture reef created out of bricks made from stabilized coal waste
Courtesy the artist

Fish Tales, 1991
20 flashcards with box and notes that document scientific research from the National Oceanic and Atmospheric Administration (NOAA) on mutated species of fish damaged by radioactive waste
colored cards 4 × 8 in.
Courtesy the artist

Mel Chin

Conditions for Memory: Passenger Pigeon, 1914, 1989
cast stone 36 × 36 × 18 in.
beech tree branch 72 × 18 × 10 in.
Courtesy the Frumkin/Adams Gallery, New York

Study for *Conditions for Memory: Passenger Pigeon, 1914*, 1989
graphite on illustration board
11 × 10 in.
Courtesy the New York City Department of Parks and Recreation

Study for *Revival Field: Hyperaccumulator Silene Cucubalis*, 1990
zinc and cadmium point on prepared ground on blotter paper, cast zinc/cadmium
20 × 20 × 2 in. (in Plexiglas box)
Courtesy Lucas and Patricia C. Johnson, Houston, Texas

Study for *Revival Field: Hyperaccumulator Festuca Rubra*, 1990
zinc and cadmium point on prepared ground on blotter paper, cast zinc/cadmium
20 × 20 × 2 in. (in Plexiglas box)
Courtesy Jody Blazek, Houston, Texas

Study for *Revival Field: Hyperaccumulator Zea Mays*, 1990
zinc and cadmium point on prepared ground on blotter paper
cast zinc/cadmium
20 × 20 × 2 in. (in Plexiglas box)
Courtesy the artist

Original plan and specifications for *Revival Field*, 1990
ink, tape, black-and-white photograph, Xerox on paper
19½ × 28¼ in.
Courtesy the artist

Maquette for *Revival Field*, 1990
steel, brass, metallic enamel, nylon, acrylic, mixed-media
8 × 44 × 44 in.
Courtesy the artist

Aluminum Gate for *Revival Field*
2 poles with flanges and metal screening
9 ft. × 4 ft. × 6 in.

Jyoti Duwadi

Fragile Ecologies: Artists' Interpretations and Solutions, 1992
Video, 15 minutes

Cheri Gaulke; Susan Boyle; and Wilson High School students Susan Barron, Jose Esquivel, Leonard Martinez, and Manuel Ortega

L.A. River Project, 1989
12 video monitors, each 20 in.
1 video monitor for narrative footage
text panel with map and photographs, 30 × 40 in.
Courtesy the artists

Helen Mayer Harrison and Newton Harrison

Survival Piece #5: Portable Orchard, 1972
photograph of installation at the Art Gallery, California State University, Fullerton
16 × 20 in.
Courtesy the artists

Drawing for *Survival Piece #5: Portable Orchard*, redrawn 1977 (after an earlier drawing)
pencil on vellum
28½ × 38½ in.
Courtesy John Hallmark Neff, Chicago, Illinois

Catalogue of the Exhibition

Outcomes (consisting of 36 photographs of
   Survival Pieces #1–7 installations), 1977
28½ x 50½ in.
Courtesy John Hallmark Neff,
   Chicago, Illinois

The Book of the Seven Lagoons, 1972–82
Hand-colored sepia-toned photographs and
   text (Edition of 31)
21½ x 28 x 2½ in. (closed) 21½ x 50½ x 6 in.
   (open)
Courtesy Ronald Feldman Fine Arts,
   New York

Breathing Space for the Sava River, Yugoslavia,
   1988–90
Installation of photographs and text
125 total running feet
Courtesy Ronald Feldman Fine Arts,
   New York

Nancy Holt
Sun Tunnels, built 1973–76
Installation of 8 photographs of site-specific
   work
62 x 92 in.
Courtesy the artist

Dark Star Park, Rosslyn, Virginia, built
   1979–84
Installation of 12 photographs of site-specific
   work
58 x 150 in.
Courtesy the artist

Sky Mound, Meadowlands, New Jersey,
   1985–present
57 acres; height 100 ft.
5 drawings
graphite on paper
Courtesy the artist

*Sky Mound Rendering: Sun-viewing area with
   pond and star-viewing mounds*, 1985
23⅛ x 47½ in.

Sky Mound Rendering: Moon-viewing area,
   1985
21 x 44½ in.

Sky Mound Rendering: Moon-viewing area
   (detail), 1985
21 x 44½ in.

*Sky Mound Rendering: Sun-viewing area seen
   from New Jersey Turnpike*, 1985
23½ x 47½ in.

*Sky Mound Rendering: Sunrise on the
   Equinoxes*, 1985
23½ x 30 in.

Sky Mound: Site plan, 1986
35 x 41 in.
Courtesy the artist

Sky Mound, 1985
color photograph
26⅛ x 40 in.
Courtesy the artist

Patricia Johanson
Butterfly Parks with Jetties, 1969
colored pencil on paper
8½ x 11 in.
Courtesy the artist

Garden Cities: Turtle Mound, 1969
pencil and ink on paper
8½ x 11 in.
Courtesy the artist

Ocean-Water Gardens, 1969
pencil on paper
8½ x 11 in.
Courtesy the artist

Water Gardens: Flood Basin and Waterfalls,
   1969
pencil on paper
8½ x 11 in.
Courtesy the artist

Leonhardt Lagoon, Dallas, Texas (originally
   called *Fair Park Lagoon*), 1981–86
3 photographs by William Pankey, each
   16 x 20 in.
Courtesy the artist

Fair Park Lagoon: Site Plan, 1982
ink on paper
13 x 26 in.
Courtesy the artist

*Fair Park Lagoon: Saggitaria Platyphylla —
   Planting Plan*, 1982
conte crayon, ink, pastel on paper
36 x 30 in.
Courtesy the artist

Fair Park Lagoon: Pteris Multifida — Planting Plan, 1982
conte crayon, ink, pastel on paper
30 × 36 in.
Courtesy the artist

Endangered Garden: Site Plans, Candlestick Cove, San Francisco Bay, California, 1988
acrylic and ink on paper
3 drawings, each 22 × 32½ in.
Courtesy the artist

Endangered Garden: Arbor, Candlestick Cove, San Francisco, California, 1988
ink on paper
Courtesy the artist

Endangered Garden: Ribbon Worm Tidal Steps, 1988
bronze
25 × 30 × 10 in.
Courtesy the artist

Heather McGill and John Roloff
Site drawing of *Isla de Umunnum* (Island of the Hummingbirds), Elkhorn Slough, Moss Landing, California, 1986
colored pencil on brown line
30 × 64 in.
Courtesy John Roloff, Oakland, California

Site/structure drawing of *Isla de Umunnum* (Island of the Hummingbirds), 1986
colored pencil on brown line
30 × 64 in.
Courtesy John Roloff, Oakland, California

Carousel tray of 80 slides documenting the project

6 black-and-white photographs of *Isla de Umunnum* sculptures and site by Michael Kenna, each 16 × 20 in.
Courtesy Stephen Wirtz Gallery, San Francisco, California

Trellis Sculpture by John Roloff and Heather McGill, Elkhorn Slough, 1989

National Refractories, Moss Landing, Study One, 1987

Moss Landing Power Station, Study Two, 1987

Midden Sculpture by John Roloff and Heather McGill, Elkhorn Slough, 1989

Eucalyptus Grove, Elkhorn Slough, 1989

Cloud Trails, Elkhorn Slough, 1989

Buster Simpson
Pharmaceutical Treatment at the Headwaters of the Hudson River, 1990, from *River Rolaids* or *Tums for Nature*, 1983–present
color photograph
16 × 20 in.
Courtesy the artist

Host Analog, rendering for Oregon Convention Center, Portland, 1991
colored xerox of drawing laminated in plastic
15 × 66 in.
Courtesy the artist

Buster Simpson, Mark Spitzer, Laura Sindell, and Becca Hanson
King Street Gardens: View from Metro Station, 1991
Ink on mylar with collaged transparencies
24 × 36 in.
Courtesy Mark Spitzer, Seattle, Washington

King Street Gardens: View of Topiary, 1991
ink on mylar with collaged transparencies
24 × 36 in.
Courtesy Mark Spitzer, Seattle, Washington

King Street Gardens: View of Hanging Garden, 1991
ink on mylar with collaged transparencies
24 × 36 in.
Courtesy Mark Spitzer, Seattle, Washington

King Street Gardens: Section of Sunken Garden, Topiary and Hanging Garden, 1991
ink on mylar with collaged transparencies
24 × 66 in.
Courtesy Mark Spitzer, Seattle, Washington

Alan Sonfist
Trinity River Time Landscape, Dallas, Texas, 1982
Photography, collage, colored pencil, and pastel
18 × 36 in.
Courtesy the artist

Time Landscape: Greenwich Village, New York, conceived mid 1960s and planted in 1978
2 reversed blueprints, each 24 × 36 in.
2 documentary photographs, each 16 × 20 in.
Courtesy the artist

Natural/Cultural History of Paris: A Narrative Environmental Landscape, 1991
photographic process and hand coloring
42½ x 180 in.
Courtesy the artist

Natural/Cultural History of Paris (cross section), 1991
photographic process and hand coloring
25 x 180 in.
Courtesy the artist

Mierle Laderman Ukeles
Sidewalk Washing Performance, SoHo, New York City, July 15, 1974
black-and-white photograph
16 x 20 in.
Courtesy Ronald Feldman Fine Arts, New York

The Social Mirror, 1983
black-and-white photograph
16 x 20 in.
Courtesy Ronald Feldman Fine Arts, New York

Flow City, 1983–present
5 drawings of permanent installation at the New York City Department of Sanitation Marine Transfer Station
Courtesy Ronald Feldman Fine Arts, New York

Overall Plan/The Three Components of Flow City: Passage Ramp/Glass Bridge/Media Flow Wall, 1992
mixed media on paper
36 x 60 in.

Passage Ramp Diptych (First Component of Flow City), 1992
mixed media with photographs of artist's related sculptures
54 x 60 in.

Glass Bridge Triptych: Three Windows on Reality (Second and Third Components of Flow City), 1992
mixed media on paper
3 drawings, each 36 x 60 in.

List of Illustrations

The Lagoon Cycle: Sixth Lagoon
from *The Book of the Seven Lagoons*, 1972–82
Hand-colored sepia-toned photographs and
    text, 21½ x 28½ in.
Photo: Courtesy Ronald Feldman Fine Arts,
    New York
FIG. 60

The Lagoon Cycle: Seventh Lagoon
from *The Book of the Seven Lagoons*, 1972–82
Hand-colored sepia-toned photographs and
    text, 21½ x 28½ in.
Photo: Courtesy Ronald Feldman Fine Arts,
    New York
FIG. 61

Breathing Space for the Sava River, Yugoslavia
"Then travels through mountains" (detail),
    1988–90
2 photo collages and text, 71¼ x 31¼ in. and
    71½ x 24 in.
Photo: Courtesy Ronald Feldman Fine Arts,
    New York
FIG. 62

Breathing Space for the Sava River, Yugoslavia
"To the alluvial flood plain" (detail), 1988–90
2 photo collages and text, 18 x 55 in. and
    15½ x 66 in.
Photo: Courtesy Ronald Feldman Fine Arts,
    New York
FIG. 63

Hogue, Alexander
Mother Earth Laid Bare, 1938
Oil on canvas, 44 x 56 in.
The Philbrook Museum of Art,
    Tulsa, Oklahoma
Photo: E. G. Schempf
FIG. 31

Holt, Nancy
Sun Tunnels, built 1973–76
Sunset Summer Solstice (detail)
Photo: Courtesy the artist
FIG. 73a

Sun Tunnels, built 1973–76
Lucin, Utah
Total length: 86 ft.; tunnels: 18 ft.
Photo: Courtesy the artist
FIG. 73b

Dark Star Park, built 1979–84
Rosslyn, Arlington, Virginia
Aerial view, ⅔ acre; gunite spheres: 6½ ft. and
    8 ft.; large tunnels: 10 x 25 ft. and 3 x 15 ft.;
    pools: 15 ft. and 18 ft.
Photo: Courtesy the artist
FIG. 74

Dark Star Park (detail), built 1979–84
Rosslyn, Arlington, Virginia
Photo: Courtesy the artist
FIG. 75

Site of *Sky Mound*, 1986
Meadowlands, New Jersey
57 acres; height 100 ft.
Photo: Courtesy the artist
FIG. 76

*Sky Mound Rendering: Sun-viewing area with
    pond and star-viewing mounds*, 1985
Graphite on paper, 23½ x 47½ in.
Photo: Courtesy the artist
FIG. 77

Sky Mound Rendering: Sunrise on the equinoxes,
    1985
Graphite on paper, 23½ x 30 in.
Photo: Courtesy the artist
FIG. 78

Sky Mound Rendering: Moon-viewing area,
    1985
Graphite on paper, 28½ x 50¼ in.
Photo: Courtesy the artist
FIG. 79

Hsü Tao-ning
Detail from *Fishermen* (Yü-fu), ca. 1000
Handscroll, ink and color on silk, 19 x 82½ in.
The Nelson-Atkins Museum of Art, Kansas
    City, Missouri (Nelson Fund) 33-1559
FIG. 13

Johanson, Patricia
Garden Cities: Turtle Mound, 1969
Ink and pencil on paper, 8½ x 11 in.
Photo: Courtesy the artist
FIG. 38

Cyrus Field (detail), 1971
Near Buskirk, New York
Cement block section, 3200 ft. long
Photo: Courtesy the artist
FIG. 52

Leonhardt Lagoon, Dallas, Texas (originally
  called *Fair Park Lagoon*), 1981–86
View of *Saggitaria Platyphylla*
Gunite, 235 × 175 × 12 ft.
Photo: William Pankey
Fig. 53

Leonhardt Lagoon, Dallas, Texas, 1981–86
Saggitaria Platyphylla (detail)
Gunite
Photo: William Pankey
Fig. 54

*Fair Park Lagoon: Saggitaria Platyphylla
  Planting Plan*, 1982
Conte Crayon, ink, pastel on paper, 36 × 30 in.
Photo: Courtesy the artist
Fig. 55

Endangered Garden, 1988–present
Sunnydale Pump Station, Candlestick Cove,
San Francisco, California
Site plan, 1988
3 drawings, acrylic and ink, each 22 × 32½ in.
Photo: Courtesy San Francisco Arts
  Commission
Fig. 56

Endangered Garden
Site plan (detail), 1988
Acrylic and ink, 22 × 32½ in.
Photo: Courtesy San Francisco Arts
  Commission
Fig. 57

Lange, Dorothea
from *An American Exodus: A Record of Human
  Erosion in the Thirties*, 1939
Black-and-white photograph
Photo: U.S. Farm Security Administration
  Collection, Prints and Photographs
  Division, Library of Congress
Fig. 29

Lorenzetti, Ambrogio
*Effects of Good Government in the City and
  Country* (detail of scenes in the countryside),
  1337-39
Fresco
Sala dei Nove, Palazzo Pubblico, Siena
Photo: Scala/Art Resource, New York
Fig. 16

McGill, Heather
Untitled, 1987
Crow Canyon Institute, San Ramon,
  California
Steel armature, passion fruit vine, white
  flowering ground cover, star jasmine and
  white oyster shells
Photo: Courtesy the artist
Fig. 92

McGill, Heather and John Roloff
Isla de Umunnum (Island of the
  Hummingbirds), 1986–90
Mound sculpture
Photo: Courtesy John Roloff
Fig. 93

Isla de Umunnum (Island of the
  Hummingbirds), 1986–90
Mound sculpture
Photo: Courtesy John Roloff
Fig. 94

Mendieta, Ana
Birth (Nacimiento), 1982
Gunpowder-Silueta series (Serie silueta de
  polvora)
Earth-body work with gunpowder
Photo: Courtesy Galerie Lelong, New York
Fig. 32

Moran, Thomas
Grand Canyon of the Yellowstone, 1872
Oil on canvas, 84 × 144¼ in.
National Museum of American Art,
  Smithsonian Institution, Lent by the U.S.
  Department of the Interior, Office of the
  Secretary
Fig. 23

Nenner, Paulette
Crucified Coyote, 1981
Sculpture installation for the *Animals in the
  Arsenal* exhibition at the Arsenal Gallery,
  Central Park, New York
Photo: Lisa Kahane
Fig. 15

Giovanni di Paolo
*The Creation of the World and the Expulsion
  from Paradise* (predella panel), 1445
Tempera and gold on panel, 18¹⁵⁄₁₆ × 20½ in.
The Metropolitan Museum of Art, Robert
  Lehman Collection, 1975
Fig. 14

Bingham Copper Mining Pit—Utah Reclamation Project, 1973
Wax pencil, tape, plastic overlay and map, 20½ x 30½ in.
Collection Elmer Johnson
Photo: Gregory W. Schmitz, New York
FIG. 40

Sonfist, Alan

Crystal Monument, 1966–72
Lucite globe with crystals, diameter 4 ft.
Photo: Courtesy the artist
FIG. 36

Earth Paintings, 1976–77
Installation at ARCO headquarters, Houston, Texas
Mixed media, 30 x 10 ft.
Photo: Courtesy the artist
FIG. 69

View of *Time Landscape: Greenwich Village, New York*, conceived mid 1960s and planted 1978
Native trees, shrubs, wildflowers
Photo: Courtesy the artist
FIG. 70a

Site plan of *Time Landscape: Greenwich Village, New York*
Reversed blueprint, 24 x 36 in.
Photo: Courtesy the artist
FIG. 70b

Trinity River Time Landscape, Dallas, Texas, 1982
Photography, collage, colored pencil, and pastel, 18 x 36 in.
Photo: Courtesy the artist
FIG. 71

Natural/Cultural History of Paris: A Narrative Environmental Landscape (detail), 1991
Photographic process and hand coloring, 42½ x 180 in.
Photo: Courtesy the artist
FIG. 72

Ukeles, Mierle Laderman

Sidewalk Washing Performance, June 15, 1974
SoHo, New York City
Photo: Courtesy Ronald Feldman Fine Arts, New York
FIG. 64

The Social Mirror, 1983
Tempered hand-fitted glass mirrors and Plexiglas on 20 cubic-yard garbage collection truck
Photo: Courtesy Ronald Feldman Fine Arts, New York
FIG. 65

Flow City, 1983–present
Installation for the Marine Transfer Station, New York City Department of Sanitation
Mixed-media drawing showing plan and video camera angles, 25 x 37 in.
Photo: D. James Dee. Courtesy Ronald Feldman Fine Arts, New York
FIG. 66

Flow City, 1983–present
Color photograph of the artist on the "Glass Bridge" at the Marine Transfer Station, New York City Department of Sanitation
Photo: Daniel Dutka
FIG. 67

Flow City, 1983–present
"Media Flow Wall"
Mixed-media drawing, 31 x 41 in.
Photo: Courtesy Ronald Feldman Fine Arts, New York
FIG. 68

Bibliography

Art

Alloway, Lawrence. "Art." *Nation* 219 (December 21, 1974): 670. (One of the first critics to address the differences between ecological and earth art.)

Antin, David. "Lead Kindly Blight." *ARTnews* 69 (November 1970).

Auping, Michael. *Common Ground: Five Artists in the Florida Landscape.* Exh. cat. The John and Mable Ringling Museum of Art, Sarasota, Fl., 1982.

Balken, Debra Bricker. *Patricia Johanson: Drawings and Models for Environmental Projects.* Exh. cat. The Berkshire Museum, Pittsfield, Mass., 1987.

Beardsley, John. *Earthworks and Beyond.* New York: Abbeville Press, 1989.

Burnham, Linda Frye. "Between the Diaspora and the Crinoline." An Interview with Bonnie Sherk. *High Performance* (Fall 1981): 49–71.

Cikovsky Jr., Nicolai. "The Ravages of the Axe: The Meaning of the Tree Stump in Nineteenth-Century American Art." *Art Bulletin* LXI (December 1979): 611–626.

Elements of Art: Earth, Air and Fire. Exh. cat. Museum of Fine Arts, Boston, 1971.

Thomas Cole: The Collected Essays and Prose Sketches. Ed. by Marshall B. Tymn. St. Paul, Minn.: John Colet Press, 1980.

Thomas Cole's Poetry. Ed. by Marshall B. Tymn. York, Pa.: Liberty Cap Books, 1972.

Delong, Lea Rosen. *Nature's Forms/Nature's Forces: The Art of Alexander Hogue.* Exh. cat. Philbrook Art Center and the University of Oklahoma Press. 1984.

"Earthkeeping/Earthshaking: Feminism and Ecology." Special issue. *Heresies* 4 (1981).

Earthworks: Land Reclamation as Sculpture, essay by Robert Morris. Exh. cat. Seattle Art Museum, 1979.

Elsen, Albert E. *Purposes of Art.* 2nd ed. New York: Holt, Rinehart & Winston, 1967.

Fort, Ilene Susan and Michael Quick. *American Art: The Los Angeles County Museum of Art Collection.* Cat. Los Angeles County Museum of Art, 1991.

Hans Haacke: Unfinished Business. Exh. cat. The New Museum of Contemporary Art. Cambridge, Mass.: MIT Press, 1986.

Harrison, Helen Mayer & Newton. *The Lagoon Cycle.* Exh. cat. Herbert F. Johnson Museum of Art, Cornell University, Ithaca, New York, 1985.

_____. *Attempause fur den Save-Fluss.* Exh. cat. Berlin: Neuer Berliner Kunstverein, 1989.

Hobbs, Robert. "Earthworks Past and Present." *Art Journal* 42 (Fall 1982): 91–94.

_____. *Robert Smithson: Sculpture.* Ithaca, New York: Cornell University Press, 1981.

Holt, Nancy, ed. *The Writings of Robert Smithson.* New York: New York University Press, 1979.

Johanson, Patricia. (Statement about her work) *Gallerie.* (1989 Annual): 20–27.

Patricia Johanson: A Selected Retrospective 1959–1973. Exh. cat. Bennington College, Bennington, Vermont, 1973.

Patricia Johanson: Public Landscapes. Exh. cat. Painted Bride Art Center, Philadelphia, Pa., 1991

Kelly, Franklin, et al. *Frederic Edwin Church.* Exh. cat. National Gallery of Art, Washington, D.C., 1989.

Knode, Marilu. *Betty Beaumont: Changing Landscapes: Art in an Expanded Field.* Exh. cat. Rochdale Art Gallery, Lancashire, England, 1989.

Lange, Dorothea, and Paul Schuster Taylor. *An American Exodus: A Record of Human Erosion in the Thirties*. Published for the Oakland Museum. New Haven: Yale University Press, 1969 (First published 1939).

Lee, Sherman E. *A History of Far Eastern Art*. New York: Harry N. Abrams, 1973.

Leroi-Gourhan, André. *Treasures of Prehistoric Art*. New York: Harry N. Abrams, 1967.

LeVeque, Terry Ryan. "Nancy Holt's 'Sky Mound': Adaptive Technology Creates Celestial Perspectives." *Landscape Architecture* (April/May, 1988): 82–86.

Lippard, Lucy. *Overlay*. New York: Pantheon, 1983.

Lovelace, Cary. "Nancy Holt Brings the Heavens Down to Earth." *Arts; New Jersey*. New Jersey Council on the Arts (Fall, 1987): 10–14.

McShine, Kynaston, ed. *The Natural Paradise: Painting in America 1800–1950*. Exh. cat. The Museum of Modern Art, New York, 1976.

Ana Mendieta: A Retrospective. Exh. cat. The New Museum of Contemporary Art, New York, 1987.

Murray, Ann. "Pits and Pitfalls: Harriet Feigenbaum's Reclamation Art." *Woman's Art Journal* (Spring/Summer, 1991): 29–36.

Novak, Barbara. *Nature and Culture*. New York: Oxford University Press, 1980.

Olmsted, Jr., Frederick Law and Theodora Kimball, eds. *Forty Years of Landscape Architecture: Central Park*. Cambridge, Mass.: The MIT Press, 1973.

Parry, Elwood C. *The Art of Thomas Cole: Ambition and Imagination*. Newark: University of Delaware Press, 1988.

Phillips, Patricia. "Public Art: Waste Not." *Art in America*. 77 (February 1989): 47–51.

Pompeii A.D. 1979. Vol. 1, Exh. cat. Museum of Fine Arts, Boston; The Art Institute of Chicago; Dallas Museum of Fine Arts; American Museum of Natural History, New York, 1978–79.

Princenthal, Nancy. "Synthesizing Art and Technology." *Heresies* 22 (Spring 1988): 68–71. (Analysis of Betty Beaumont's work)

Rockefeller, Steven C. and John C. Elder. *Spirit and Nature: Visions of Interdependence*. Exh. cat. Johnson Art Gallery, Middlebury College, Vermont, 1990.

Ruspoli, Mario. *The Cave of Lascaux: The Final Photographs*. New York: Harry N. Abrams, 1987.

Sandler, Irving. *American Art of the 1960s*. New York: Harper & Row, 1988.

Smith, W. Eugene and Aileen M. *Minamata*. New York: Holt, Rinehart and Winston, 1975.

Sonfist, Alan, ed. *Art in the Land*, New York: E.P. Dutton, 1983.

Alan Sonfist 1969–89, Exh. cat. Hillwood Art Museum, Long Island Univeristy, Brookville, New York, 1989. (Interview with Robert Rosenblum)

Tisdall, Caroline. *Joseph Beuys*. Exh. cat. The Solomon R. Guggenheim Museum, New York, 1979.

Truettner, William H., ed. *The West as America: Reinterpreting Images of the Frontier 1820–1920*. Exh. cat. The National Museum of American Art. Washington, D.C.: The Smithsonian Institution Press, 1991.

Tsai, Eugenie. *Robert Smithson Unearthed: Drawings, Collages, Writings*. New York: Columbia University Press, 1991.

Ukeles, Mierle Laderman. "Manifesto! Maintenance Art." *Idea Art*. Gregory Battcock, ed. New York: E.P. Dutton, 1973.

Wade, Edwin. *The Arts of the North American Indian*. New York: Hudson Hills Press, 1986.

Wardwell, Allen. *Objects of Bright Pride: Northwest Coast Indian Art from the American Museum of Natural History*. 2nd ed. rev. Washington: University of Washington Press, 1988.

Environmental Studies, Literature, Mythology, Philosophy

Anderson, William and Clive Hicks. *Green Man: The Archetype of Our Oneness with the Earth*. London: HarperCollins, 1990.

Berger, John. *Restoring the Earth*. New York: Doubleday, 1987.

Berry, Thomas. *The Dream of the Earth*. San Francisco: Sierra Club Books, 1990.

Berry, Wendell. *The Unsettling of America*. San Francisco: Sierra Club Books, 1977.

Black Elk Speaks, trans. by John G. Niehardt. Lincoln: University of Nebraska Press, 1961.

Brown, Lester, et al., ed. *State of the World 1989*. (also edns. 1990 and 1991) New York: W.W. Norton, 1989, 1990, 1991.

Campbell, Joseph (with Bill Moyers). *The Power of Myth*. New York: Doubleday, 1988.

_____. *The Mythic Image*. Princeton, N.J.: Princeton University Press, 1974.

_____. *The Masks of God: Primitive Mythology*, New York: Penguin Books, 1987.

Carson, Rachel. *Silent Spring*. Boston: Houghton Mifflin, 1962.

Chan, Wing-Tsit, trans. and comp. *A Source Book in Chinese Philosophy*. Princeton, N.J.: Princeton University Press, 1963.

Chekhov, Anton. *Anton Chekhov's Plays*, trans. and ed. by Eugene K. Bristow. New York: W.W. Norton, 1977.

Commoner, Barry. *The Closing Circle: Nature, Man and Technology*. New York: Alfred A. Knopf, 1975.

Devall, Bill and George Sessions. *Deep Ecology*. Salt Lake City: Gibbs Smith, 1985.

Eliade, Mircea, ed. *The Encyclopedia of Religion*, 16 vols. New York: Macmillan, 1987.

Finch, Robert and John Elder, eds. *The Norton Book of Nature Writing*. New York: W. W. Norton, 1990.

Frazer, James George. *The Golden Bough*. Vol. 1 (abridged ed.). New York: Macmillan, 1963.

Friday, Laurie, and Ronald Laskey, eds. *The Fragile Environment, The Darwin College Lectures*. Cambridge: Cambridge University Press, 1989.

Gallenkamp, Charles. *Maya*. New York: Penguin Books, 1987.

Gimbutas, Marija. *The Language of the Goddess*. London: Thames & Hudson, 1989.

Global Tomorrow Coalition. *The Global Ecology Handbook*. Boston: Beacon Press, 1990.

Jackson, Wes. *New Roots for Agriculture*. San Francisco: Friends of the Earth, 1980.

Leopold, Aldo. *A Sand County Almanac*. New York: Oxford University Press, 1949.

Marsh, George Perkins. *Man and Nature*. New York: Charles Scribner, 1864.

Marx, Leo. *The Machine in the Garden: Technology and the Pastoral Ideal in America*. New York: Oxford University Press, 1964.

Merchant, Carolyn. *The Death of Nature: Women, Ecology and the Scientific Revolution*. San Francisco: HarperCollins, 1983.

Mumford, Lewis. The City in History. New York: Harcourt, Brace & World, 1961.

Myers, Norman, ed. *Gaia: An Atlas of Planet Management.* Garden City: Anchor Press/Doubleday, 1984.

Nash, Roderick Frazier. *Wilderness and the American Mind.* 3rd ed. New Haven, Conn.: Yale University Press, 1982.

———. *The Rights of Nature: A History of Environmental Ethics.* Madison: The University of Wisconsin Press, 1989.

———. *American Environmentalism: Readings in Conservation History.* 3rd ed. New York: McGraw Hill, 1990.

Nebel, Bernard J. *Environmental Science: The Way the World Works.* 3rd ed. Englewood Cliffs, N.J.: Prentice-Hall, 1990.

Neumann, Erich *The Great Mother: An Analysis of an Archetype.* Trans. by Ralph Manheim. Bollingen Series XLVI. Princeton, New Jersey: Princeton University Press, 1972.

Reader, John. *Mankind on Earth.* New York: Harper & Row, 1988.

Riis, Jacob A. *How the Other Half Lives: Studies Among the Tenements of New York.* New York: Dover Publications, 1971. (First published 1890)

Schell, Jonathan. *The Fate of the Earth.* New York: Avon Books, 1982.

Schumacher, E. F. *Small is Beautiful.* New York: Harper & Row, 1973. (Reprinted 1989)

Schweitzer, Albert. *The Teaching of Reverence for Life.* New York: Holt, Rinehart and Winston, 1965.

Sen, N. B. *Wit and Wisdom of Gandhi, Nehru, Tagore.* New Delhi: New Book Society of India, 1968.

Silberstein, Mark, and Eileen Campbell. *Elkhorn Slough.* Monterey, Calif.: Monterey Bay Aquarium, 1989.

Simmons, I. G. *Changing the Face of the Earth.* Oxford: Basil Blackwell, 1989.

Snyder, Gary. *Turtle Island.* New York: New Directions Books, 1974

Stryk, Lucien, and Takashi Ikemoto, ed. and trans., *The Penguin Book of Zen Poetry.* London: Penguin Books, 1987.

Thomas, Keith. *Man and the Natural World.* New York: Pantheon Books, 1983.

Thoreau, Henry D. *Walden or Life in the Woods.* Garden City, N.Y.: Dolphin Books, 1960. (First published 1854)

Weiner, Jonathan. *The Next One Hundred Years.* New York: Bantam, 1990.

Wilson, Edward O. *Biophilia: The human bond with other species.* Cambridge, Mass.: Harvard University Press, 1984.

World Resources 1990–91: A Guide to the Global Environment. The World Resources Institute in collaboration with the United Nations Environment Programme and the United Nations Development Programme. New York and Oxford: Oxford University Press, 1990.

Worster, Donald. *Dust Bowl: The Southern Plains in the 1930's.* New York: Oxford University Press, 1979.

Index

The Queens Museum of Art